Science Fair Projects
Volume 2
Middle School

D1476582

by
Lesa L. Rohrer

Published by Milestone
an imprint of
Frank Schaffer Publications®

Author: Lesa L. Rohrer
Editors: Cary Malaski, Diana Wallis

Frank Schaffer Publications®

Milestone is an imprint of Frank Schaffer Publications.

Send all inquiries to:
Frank Schaffer Publications
3195 Wilson Drive NW
Grand Rapids, Michigan 49544

Science Fair Projects: Volume 2—middle school

ISBN 0-7696-3429-X

2 3 4 5 6 7 8 9 10 PAT 10 09 08 07 06

Table of Contents

{ Introduction

Science fair—when spoken in a classroom or curriculum meeting, these two words can create a wide range of emotions. Some sigh and exclaim, "Oh, no! Not again!" Others proclaim, "Oh, boy, I can't wait to get started!" No matter which side of the fence you're on, a science fair allows students to explore scientific inquiry. Their hands-on projects promote scientific literacy by engaging them in the science process.

Science fairs vary from school to school in the level of competition. But the importance of science fairs is in students learning to move beyond simple recall using someone else's information and entering an environment that encourages them to ask their own questions. They use the scientific method to accumulate information from which they can derive answers to their questions. A science fair encourages students in a particular way of thinking and processing information. This cognition extends to other areas as students become more aware of the world around them. In addition, students will begin to see science as a multistepped process instead of a book of facts. Because the experiments generally extend over a period of time, students learn that finding answers involves both patience and a proper method of data collection.

This book provides science fair project ideas for students and teachers. Experiments give step-by-step procedures based on the scientific method. This approach allows students to carry out experiments and to learn how scientists discover all those facts they read in their science textbooks.

In the beginning of the book are several pages to help students understand the steps of the scientific method, as well as how to collect and communicate data in the most appropriate format.

The "Baffling Liquid Challenge" (p. 16) gives teacher information to help you guide students through an experiment. After that, they begin working independently. Extensions and alternatives at the end of each project give students more options. The book ends with a presentation guide to help students present their findings. Even the most wonderful experiment may not receive the recognition it deserves if it is not displayed and organized in the right way.

A great way to choose experiments for the science fair is through brainstorming. Brainstorming helps the teacher discover what students are curious about. All topics mentioned during brainstorming, such as plants, cars, bugs, electricity, and even music, should be recorded. Next, ask your students to think of questions related to each topic. Questions can range from why certain bugs live in certain areas to why dogs hear higher notes than humans do. Brainstorming not only generates excitement and anticipation about the science fair, but it also helps students identify their areas of interest.

Projects in this book are classified in groups to help students narrow down their choices.

> Investigating Humans—research related to humans

> Investigating the Environment—explorations of environmental issues

> Investigating the Marketplace—projects that explore consumer choices and concerns

> Investigating the Natural World—explorations of earth, physical, and life science concepts

Encourage students to choose experiments during your individual conferences with them. This allows you to tap into individual interests so that the student will gain the most from the science fair experience. It also gives students time to investigate and choose a topic they are curious about.

Once students choose their experiments, they should read through them several times to develop questions and to evaluate potential problems. Students should have a clear idea of what they are doing before they begin. When you feel confident that each student understands the goal of her or his experiment, allow students to begin their projects with minimal supervision from you. Students should be able to do the projects in this book largely on their own. You facilitate learning by acting as a resource, enabling students to learn the most in their role as the experimenter.

Introducing The Scientific Method

The scientific method is a systematic, step-by-step way to collect data to help find the answer to a scientific question. The scientific method uses the following eight steps.

Step One } **MAKE AN OBSERVATION.** All science questions begin with noticing things happening around you by using your senses and/or making measurements.

Step Two } **STATE THE PROBLEM AND POSE IT AS A RESEARCH QUESTION.** Observations lead us to ask questions about our world. Every event can be broken into two parts—cause and effect. What you observe is the effect. Thinking about what might cause the effect can help you pose a research question. For example, Isaac Newton observed that apples falling from a tree always fell down—not up or any other direction. Apples falling down was the effect. The problem he wanted to solve was what caused them to fall down.

Step Three } **CONDUCT YOUR RESEARCH.** Once the question is posed, find out what is already known about the topic by researching books and/or the Internet. Research will give you the information you need to make a hypothesis.

Step Four } **FORMULATE A HYPOTHESIS.** A hypothesis predicts a possible answer to your research question. The independent variable is the thing you will change during the experiment. Your hypothesis will state—predict—what effect you think the independent variable will have on the dependent variable, based on your research.

The dependent variable is the part of the experiment that will be affected by what is changed. To clarify both variables, a hypothesis is usually written as an *if/then* statement. *If* I change this, *then* this is what I think will happen because . . . For example, I hypothesize (predict) that <u>if I throw apples up in the air to different heights</u>, *then they will always fall back down*, because there is a force pulling everything to the earth. The independent variable (underlined above) is the different heights to which I will throw the apples. The dependent variable (in italics above) is what I expect will happen as a result of how high I throw the apples.

Step Five } **DESIGN AND CONDUCT AN EXPERIMENT.** An experiment provides an organized way to collect data to prove or disprove a hypothesis and to answer a scientific question. An experiment is made up of the following parts.

    A. Identify variables you will keep the same—these are controlled variables.

    B. Make a list of all the materials you will use.

    C. Outline a step-by-step procedure in a clear and concise manner so that someone else could conduct the same experiment if needed. Conduct the experiment according to the steps of the procedure.

    D. Collect the data using a table.

    E. If possible, repeat the experiment at least two more times and average the data from all three experiments.

Published by Milestone. Copyright protected.

Step Six } **COMMUNICATE THE DATA IN AN APPROPRIATE MANNER.** Record the data you collect through measurements or observations in a clearly labeled data table. Use the data table to construct the appropriate type of graph to provide a pictorial representation of what happened during the experiment.

Step Seven } **ANALYZE THE RESULTS OF AN EXPERIMENT TO DRAW A CONCLUSION.** A conclusion answers the question (see steps two and four) based on analyzing the data collected during the experiment.

Step Eight } **EXPLAIN YOUR FINDINGS WITH AN INFERENCE.** An inference is a logical explanation of what happened. An inference often leads to another research question, hypothesis, and experiment.

What is so important about the scientific method? The scientific method allows a scientist to use an organized problem-solving approach to answer a question. If the scientist encounters problems, or the experiment fails, the scientific method also is a way to make logical changes to the experiment. Before the scientific method was widely used, experimenters used a trial-and-error approach that often gave them misleading results and incorrect conclusions.

The scientific method also allows scientists to repeat or replicate another scientist's work. If the experiment cannot be replicated or if it is replicated with different results, the conclusions drawn from it are suspect. In this way, the scientific method makes it possible to verify results.

Many people use the scientific method without even realizing it. Think of a chef who creates a new dessert. He first observes what kind of desserts people like. Then he questions how he can improve this dessert. He then researches to find what ingredients others have used before and experiments with his own combinations. He probably conducts taste tests to evaluate combinations before arriving at a delicious recipe based on his findings.

 0-7696-3429-X *Science Fair Projects: Volume 2*

A Guided Tour Through The Scientific Method

Step One } **MAKE AN OBSERVATION.** I observe that the same-sized beverage glasses filled with different shapes of ice hold different amounts of a liquid.

Step Two } **STATE THE PROBLEM AND POSE IT AS A RESEARCH QUESTION.** Think about cause and effect. In other words, look at the relationship between what happened and what caused it to happen.

> **Effect:** different volumes of liquid in the containers
>
> **Possible Cause:** different shapes of ice
>
> **Research Question:** How does the shape of ice added to a liquid affect the volume of the liquid in the container?

Step Three } **RESEARCH THE QUESTION.** I researched to define *volume* and to learn how volume is measured. I also researched the term *density* to see how it is related to the volume of two substances in a fixed amount of space.

Step Four } **FORMULATE A HYPOTHESIS.** I predict that if I fill a cup with cubed ice instead of smaller ice pellets, then there will be less liquid in my cup because the cubed ice will take up more space.

The independent variable—written after *if*—is what I will change. The dependent variable—written after *then*—is the part of the experiment that may be affected by what I change.

Step Five } **DESIGN AND CONDUCT AN EXPERIMENT.**

A. Identify controlled variables. same size and type of cup, ice kept in the same freezer, same method used to measure the volume of the liquid, and the same temperature of the liquid added to the cup.

B. List materials. twelve 300-ml plastic cups at room temperature, 4 different shapes of ice kept in the same freezer, one 250-ml graduated cylinder or measuring cup, cold tap water, a strainer, and data table 1.1 (p. 9)

C. Procedure
1. Buy or make 4 different shapes of ice.
2. Store ice in the freezer until it is needed.
3. Use the graduated cylinder to find out how much liquid fits into the cup before ice is added.
4. Fill another cup with one shape of ice from the freezer.
5. Let cold water run for 1 minute and then add it to the cup of ice.
6. Use a strainer to drain the water from the cup into the graduated cylinder.

Published by Milestone. Copyright protected.

7. Record the measurement in a data table.
8. Repeat steps 4–7 with other ice shapes.
9. Find the average for each shape and communicate the findings in a graph.

D. Conduct the experiment, collect data, and repeat the experiment to obtain an average.

Table 1.1 How much liquid do you get?

Volume of liquid in cup	w/ ice pellets	w/ circular ice	w/ cubed ice	w/ bagged ice
Trial 1 volume (ml)	75	135	100	132
Trial 2 volume (ml)	70	122	97	140
Trial 3 volume (ml)	78	134	92	131
Average volume (ml)	74	130	96	134

Step Six } **COMMUNICATE THE DATA IN AN APPROPRIATE MANNER.**

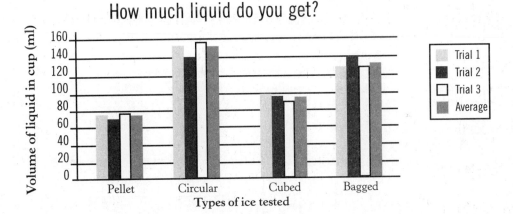

How much liquid do you get?

Step Seven } **ANALYZE THE RESULTS TO DRAW A CONCLUSION.** Based on the data, my hypothesis was not correct. The cup with cubed ice held more liquid than the cup with ice pellets. The data also shows that the cups with circular and bagged ice held about the same amount of liquid.

Step Eight } **EXPLAIN THE FINDINGS WITH AN INFERENCE.** This step explains my conclusion. Ice pellets take up more space because they are smaller and can pack together better than cubed ice. There is less room for liquid. Both circular and bagged ice take up the same amount of space because their molds are about the same size.

(9)

Graphic Communication

Graphs provide a picture of the data that is easy to understand and analyze. The type of graph you should use depends on the type of data collected. The main types of graphs used to communicate data are line and bar graphs. To better understand how and what graphs communicate, look at these examples.

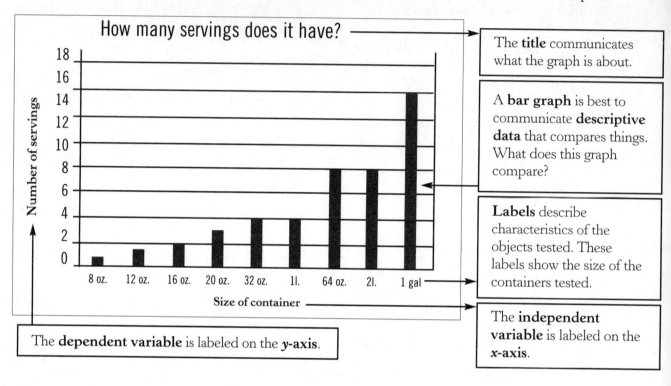

The **title** communicates what the graph is about.

A **bar graph** is best to communicate **descriptive data** that compares things. What does this graph compare?

Labels describe characteristics of the objects tested. These labels show the size of the containers tested.

The **independent variable** is labeled on the **x-axis**.

The **dependent variable** is labeled on the **y-axis**.

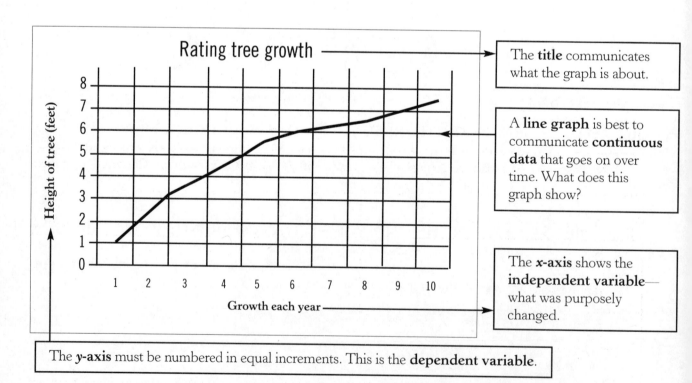

The **title** communicates what the graph is about.

A **line graph** is best to communicate **continuous data** that goes on over time. What does this graph show?

The **x-axis** shows the **independent variable**— what was purposely changed.

The **y-axis** must be numbered in equal increments. This is the **dependent variable**.

0-7696-3429-X *Science Fair Projects: Volume 2*

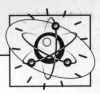

Graphic Communication (cont.)

Use the information on page 10 to answer the following questions.

1. Why are graphs often used to display data collected during an experiment? _____
    _____

2. What are the two main types of graphs used to communicate data collected during an experiment?
    _____

3. Compare: How are the two types of graphs alike? _____
    _____

4. Contrast: How do the two types of graphs differ? _____
    _____

5. Decide which type of graph should be used for the data sets described in the following table. Write your choices in the last column.

Table 1.2

Data set	Description of data	Type of graph
A	Students collected data to determine what vehicle color was most popular by comparing the number of vehicles of each color in the school parking lot.	
B	Students measured the heights of students in their classroom to compare the heights and ages.	
C	Students measured the time it took for a fizzing tablet to dissolve in different temperatures of water.	
D	Students collected data to find out which type of fast food was most popular among their classmates.	
E	Students timed how long it took different ages of students in their building to work a puzzle.	

6. For the data sets above, decide what the labels for both the *x*- and *y*-axes would be by identifying the independent and dependent variables. Then create a title. The first one has been done for you.

Table 1.3

Data set	Label on *x*-axis (independent variable)	Label on *y*-axis (dependent variable)	Title
A	Vehicle color	Number of vehicles	Which vehicle color is most popular?
B			
C			
D			
E			

0-7696-3429-X *Science Fair Projects: Volume 2*

Smarties Graphs (Understanding Graphs)

In the three investigations that follow, you will collect data and construct different types of graphs to determine how graphs communicate the results of an experiment. In procedure B, you will work with a circle graph, a third type of graph scientists sometimes use.

MATERIALS: student pages (pp. 13–14), a package of Smarties per student, a ruler, a protractor, colored pencils (optional), and a calculator

Procedure A: Smarties Colors

Type of Data: Descriptive data that compares, communicated by a bar graph

1. Open your package of Smarties and sort them according to color.
2. Record the color and the number of each color in data table A (p. 13).
3. Label and complete a graph to communicate the data. Colored pencils may be used if desired.
4. Answer the conclusion questions for this set (p. 13).

Procedure B: Smarties Percents

Type of Data: Percentages of 100, communicated by a circle graph

1. Transfer the data regarding color from table A to table B (p. 13).
2. Count the total number of Smarties in your package and record it in table B.
3. Find the percent of each color of Smarties by using the following formula:
   (Number of one color ÷ total number of Smarties) x 100. Round to nearest whole number.
4. Find the size of each part of the circle to show your data using this formula:
   360 x % of color* = degrees of circle. Round to nearest whole number.

   Hint: 360 x .15 is the same as 360 x 15%.
   *Be sure to hit the percent key after entering the number of a color.
5. Use a protractor to measure the angles for each section of the circle.
6. Create a circle graph. Label the sections with percentage and color, or use colored pencils to communicate the color of each section.
7. Answer the conclusion questions for this set (p. 13).

Procedure C: Smarties Lengths

Type of Data: Continuous data, communicated by a line graph

1. Place two Smarties end to end to start a line.
2. Measure the length of the line and record your measurement in data table C (p. 14).
3. Repeat steps 1 and 2 using 4, 6, 8, 10, and 12 Smarties. Record each measurement in the data table.
4. Construct and label a line graph to communicate this continuous data.
5. Enjoy your Smarties as you answer the conclusion questions (p. 14).

Smarties is a registered trademark of Ce De Candy Inc.

Table A — Smarties colors

No. of Smarties						
Color						

Graph A

(empty grid)

Conclusions

1. What type of data is communicated with a bar graph? _____

2. What is the independent variable shown on the graph? _____

   Where is it labeled? _____

3. What is the dependent variable? _____

   Where is it labeled? _____

Table B — Smarties percents

Color and how many						
Total number						
Percent of each color						
Angle degree of circle graph						

Graph B

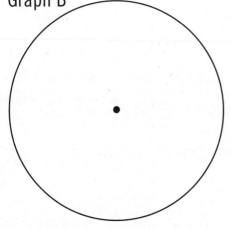

Conclusions

1. What type of data is communicated with a circle graph?

   _____

2. Which of the two graphs used for color do you think communicates the data best? _____

   _____

   Why? _____

   _____

Published by Milestone. Copyright protected.

0-7696-3429-X *Science Fair Projects: Volume 2*

Table C — Smarties lengths

Line length (cm)						
Number of Smarties	2	4	6	8	10	12

Graph C

(blank grid)

Conclusions

1. What type of data is communicated with a line graph?

   _____

2. What is the dependent variable for this set of data?

   _____

3. What is the independent variable for this set of data?

   _____

4. What would the length of three Smarties be?

   _____ 14 Smarties? _____

Questions to Consider

1. Which type of graph is easiest for you to understand? _____
   Why?_____

2. What information can a graph communicate? _____

3. On which axis is the independent variable found? _____
   The dependent variable? _____

4. What should the title on a graph communicate?_____

5. List three other examples of descriptive data that could be collected during an experiment.

6. List three other examples of continuous data that could be collected during an experiment.

7. Extension: Find a graph from a local newspaper. Glue it to a separate sheet of paper.
   Explain what the graph is communicating.

Writing a Clear Procedure

Write your procedure clearly enough for someone else to perform your experiment. A recipe in a cookbook is a good example of a procedure. It tells exactly what materials we need and provides a step-by-step guide, or instructions, to create a finished product. In this activity, you will write a step-by-step procedure using both directions and measurements to detail how to draw a geometric shape or design. Do not identify the shape or design. You will trade papers with a classmate to test how clearly your procedure is written. When the classmate gives you the drawing he or she made by following your instructions, answer the questions below.

PROCEDURE

_____

_____

_____

_____

_____

_____

_____

_____

_____

_____

_____

_____

_____

_____

_____

_____

Answer the following questions about your procedure.

1. **Conclusion:** Was your classmate's drawing correct? _____

2. **Inference:** Why do you think this happened? _____

_____

3. **Evaluation:** Why is it important to write a clear and concise procedure? _____

_____

_____

   0-7696-3429-X *Science Fair Projects: Volume 2*

The Baffling Liquid Challenge

Use pages 17–18 to give students a hands-on opportunity to use and identify the steps of the scientific method to solve a problem. Here are the materials and information you need to guide the students through the process.

Materials: 3 clear plastic cups for each group, 3 clear liquids as specified below, red and blue litmus paper, 3 pipettes or cotton swabs for each group, safety goggles, resource materials that explain acids and bases and how to test for each, and a timer

Keep the following solutions stored in clean, clear 2-liter containers:

Solution A: 2 liters of *distilled water

Solution B: 2 liters of a 0.1 molar hydrochloric acid solution

Solution C: 2 liters of a 0.1 sodium hydroxide basic solution

* Use distilled water—most tap water is slightly basic.

CAUTION: Remind students to use the wafting technique to smell the liquids and never to taste an unknown solution.

Setup. Explain the challenge to your students by showing them the three solutions in the clear containers. As students make observations regarding the solutions, you can list the observations on the board. Then have students identify the problem by stating it as a research question. Provide materials that have information on acids and bases and help students discover that acidic solutions turn blue litmus paper red, and basic solutions turn red litmus paper blue. Then, help students identify the independent and dependent variables.

Independent variable: type of solution

Dependent variable: whether the solution is safe to drink

Now your students should be able to formulate a hypothesis and design an experiment to test the hypothesis. Remind students not to contaminate the solutions while testing them. Have students brainstorm ways they can test the solutions. Also remind students to wear safety goggles because they will be working with unknown solutions. When students have formulated their hypotheses and designed their experiments, provide them with the materials they request. Allow them time to conduct the experiments and make their conclusions.

Conclusion. Solution A is safe to drink because it did not react with either the red or blue litmus paper.

The Baffling Liquid Challenge

Solve the following problem by using the steps of the scientific method. Explain each step thoroughly in the spaces provided.

Step One } **OBSERVATION.** One of three glasses of clear liquids is safe to drink.

Step Two } **PROBLEM.** You have three glasses of clear, odorless liquids. One glass contains a poisonous acid, another glass contains a toxic base, and the third glass contains a substance that is safe to drink. You will have thirty minutes to develop a test to decide which glass of liquid you can safely drink.

First, identify a possible cause and effect relationship and pose a research question.

Effect (what do you observe?): _____

Possible cause: _____

Research Question: _____

_____

Step Three } **RESEARCH.** Use resources to define the following terms.

Acid _____

_____

Base _____

_____

How can you test a liquid to determine if it is an acid or a base?

_____

Step Four } **HYPOTHESIS.** Your next step is to formulate a testable hypothesis. To do this, you must identify both the independent and dependent variables.

Independent Variable _____

Dependent Variable _____

Now formulate your hypothesis by predicting how the independent variable will affect the dependent variable. *(Hint: Remember to phrase your statement using the words* if *and* then.*)*

_____

_____

Step Five } **DESIGN AND CONDUCT AN EXPERIMENT.**

    A. **Controlled Variables:** Identify the part(s) of the experiment you will keep the same throughout.

_____

_____

    B. **Materials:**

_____

_____

    C. **Procedure:** Someone else should be able to conduct your experiment by following the steps you list.

_____

_____

_____

_____

_____

_____

    D. **Collect data:** Now conduct your experiment. Record the data you collect here.

Step Six } **COMMUNICATE DATA.** Create the appropriate type of graph to best communicate your data. Use another piece of paper.

Step Seven } **CONCLUSION.** Which liquid is safe to drink, based on the results of your experiment?

Step Eight } **INFERENCE.** Explain your results, based on your research.

(18)

Dominant Hemisphere

Step One

> **MAKE AN OBSERVATION.** Have you noticed that some people seem naturally good at math while others seem naturally good at writing a creative story? Human brains have two hemispheres—left and right. Some people say the right hemisphere processes nonverbal, concrete, and spatial information. It allows us to do creative tasks such as writing a story. They say the left hemisphere processes verbal, abstract, and analytical information, meaning that it allows us to do more analytical tasks such as solving a math problem. These people believe individuals tend to have one dominant hemisphere.

Step Two

> **STATE THE PROBLEM AND POSE IT AS A RESEARCH QUESTION.** Find a way to determine what effect an individual's brain dominance has on the way he or she learns. Many tests try to answer this question with a variety of questions and responses. Responses show dominance of the right hemisphere, the left hemisphere, or both equally. In this investigation, you will administer a brain dominance quiz to find out which hemisphere your subjects rely on most when processing information.

> > What is the effect you observe?
>
> > What is the possible cause of the effect?
>
> > How can it be posed as a research question?

Step Three

> **CONDUCT YOUR RESEARCH.** Investigate the terms *demographic study*, *brain dominance*, and *cognition*. Write a summary explaining what you find out. You can include a table to show the characteristics usually assigned to each hemisphere.

Step Four

> **FORMULATE A HYPOTHESIS.** To form a hypothesis, observe your classmates to determine which characteristics they exhibit, based on your research. When your observations have been made, formulate a hypothesis that predicts which characteristics the majority of the students you survey will display—those considered left brain, right brain, or both equally.

Step Five

> **DESIGN AND CONDUCT YOUR EXPERIMENT.**

> **A. Identify variables you will keep the same during the experiment.** Consider how your test group is demographically the same (same grade and same school). Also consider using the same test under the same conditions, and consider using the same method to score the tests given.

0-7696-3429-X *Science Fair Projects: Volume 2*

INVESTIGATING HUMANS

B. Materials: 30 people, 30 consent forms, 30 copies of brain quiz (pp. 22–23), circle graph (p. 24), and quiz evaluation (table 2.1 below)

C. Procedure

1. Select 30 classmates to survey. Get their written consents (p. 21) to participate in this survey.

2. Arrange a time for each participant to take the brain quiz on pages 22–23.

3. Use the information in table 2.1 below to evaluate each individual's responses. Mark an *L* for left, an *R* for right, or a *B* for both beside each question, according to the participant's answers.

4. Count the number of questions with *L*, *R* and *B*.

5. Decide which hemisphere each individual relies on most based on her or his totals. Record it in the space at the end of the quiz. If a person's numbers for both left and right are the same, record dominance as equal.

6. Use table 2.2 at the bottom of this page to find the total number of students who seem to show dominance of each hemisphere by placing a tally mark for each student in the correct column.

D. Collect data.

Table 2.1   Quiz evaluation

Question	Left	Right	Both	Question	Left	Right	Both
1	a	b	c	14	a	b	
2	a, b	c		15	b	a	
3	a, b	c		16	a	b	
4	c	a, b		17	a	b	
5	b	a		18	b	a	
6	b	a, c		19	a	b	
7	b, c	a		20	a	b	
8	a	b, c		21	b	a	
9	b	a		22	a	b	
10	b	a, c		23	b	a	
11	a	b		24	a	b	
12	a	b		25	b	a	
13	b	a					

Table 2.2   Tabulate results

Dominant hemisphere	Left	Right	Equal
Number of students with dominance			

0-7696-3429-X *Science Fair Projects: Volume 2*

Step Six } **COMMUNICATE YOUR DATA IN AN APPROPRIATE MANNER.**
Use the circle graph on page 24 to report percentages of students that show each type of brain dominance. Use the formula and table 2.3 below to calculate the part of a circle graph each number represents. Remember that there are 360° in a circle so each part will be measured in degrees. Label the circle graph and use colored pencils.

$$(n \div y) \times 360° = d°,$$

in which n = number of students per dominance, y = total surveyed (30), and d = degrees of a circle.

Table 2.3 Calculate parts of a circle *(Round your answer to the nearest whole number.)*

Hemi dominance	Left	Right	Equal
n			
$\div y$	$\div 30 =$	$\div 30 =$	$\div 30 =$
x 360	x 360°	x 360°	x 360°
$= d$			

Step Seven } **ANALYZE THE RESULTS TO DRAW A CONCLUSION.** Based on your data, write a conclusion statement that summarizes your findings (how many people surveyed had each dominance), explains what your data means (characteristics of each dominance), and identifies how your data could be used to help students learn better.

Step Eight } **EXPLAIN YOUR FINDINGS WITH AN INFERENCE.** Logically explain why the results came out as they did. Remember, an inference may lead to another question or experiment.

Alternatives and extensions

1. Change the survey group to determine if age has an effect on brain dominance by choosing participants from different age groups. Follow the same procedure to collect your data.

2. Locate another test used to determine brain dominance. Administer both tests to the same group of subjects to determine if both tests yield the same results.

Consent: Dominant Hemis

I consent to take part in a study to determine which side of my brain I rely on most to process information. I understand that the results of my survey will be used as data in a science fair project. I also understand that my name will not be used or published.

Printed name of participant _____

Signature_____ Date _____

Left Brain/Right Brain Quiz

Circle the best answer.

1. Which of the following words do you like best?
   a. titillating
   b. syzygy
   c. jujube

2. Which number sequence makes the most sense to you?
   a. 1   3   5
   b. 1   3   4
   c. 1   3   1   4

3. *A* is related to *US* in somewhat the same way as
   a. *C* is related to *AB*.
   b. *The* is related to *Them*.
   c. *Z* is related to *EG*.

4. The relationship between walk and dance is most like the relationship between
   a. slow and fast.
   b. climb and jump.
   c. run and march.

5. I prefer
   a. putting together a jigsaw puzzle.
   b. doing a crossword puzzle.

6.
   is to as
   a. is to .
   b. 3 is to 5.
   c. is to .

7. *I* and *M* together is most like
   a. *U* and *R*.
   b. 9 and 13.
   c. *O* and *S*.

8. The relationship between *sing/song* can best be described by the following word pair:
   a. *verb/noun*.
   b. *ping/pong*.
   c. *write/book*.

9. When I hear or see the word *blue*, I associate it with
   a. being sad.
   b. the color.

10. The pair that best matches the relationship between 15 and 6 is
    a. 23 and 5.
    b. 23 and 8.
    c. higher and lower.

11. I usually decide what I will wear to school
    a. the night before.
    b. when I get up.

12. When my mother calls me, I respond most to
    a. her words.
    b. the tone of her voice.

13. I prefer to
    a. draw and color my own picture.
    b. color a picture that is already drawn.

14. The following statement best describes me:
   a. I am usually on time.
   b. I am usually running late.

15. When I know that I have a free Saturday I usually
   a. just see what pops up.
   b. plan my day to get things done.

16. When trying to learn something for the first time, I prefer
   a. to be told how to do it.
   b. to be shown how to do it.

17. In English class, I prefer
   a. reading a story and writing a summary of its meaning in my own words.
   b. reading a story and answering a set of questions.

18. In school, I prefer
   a. solving a problem with no set answer.
   b. following a procedure to arrive at a set answer.

19. At home, my room is
   a. neat with everything in its own place.
   b. what some would call a disaster area, but I know where things are.

20. I work best
   a. by myself.
   b. in a group.

21. When talking,
   a. I use my hands a lot.
   b. I hardly ever use my hands.

22. I best remember
   a. people's names.
   b. people's faces.

23. I prefer to study or to do my homework
   a. in a place with some background noise.
   b. in a place that is quiet.

24. I prefer to organize information
   a. by using a table or outline.
   b. by using a web or just jotting down pieces of information.

25. I am most comfortable
   a. in a large group of people.
   b. in a small group of close friends.

Total left _____

Total right _____

Total both _____

Dominance _____

Published by Milestone. Copyright protected.

Student brain-dominance percentages

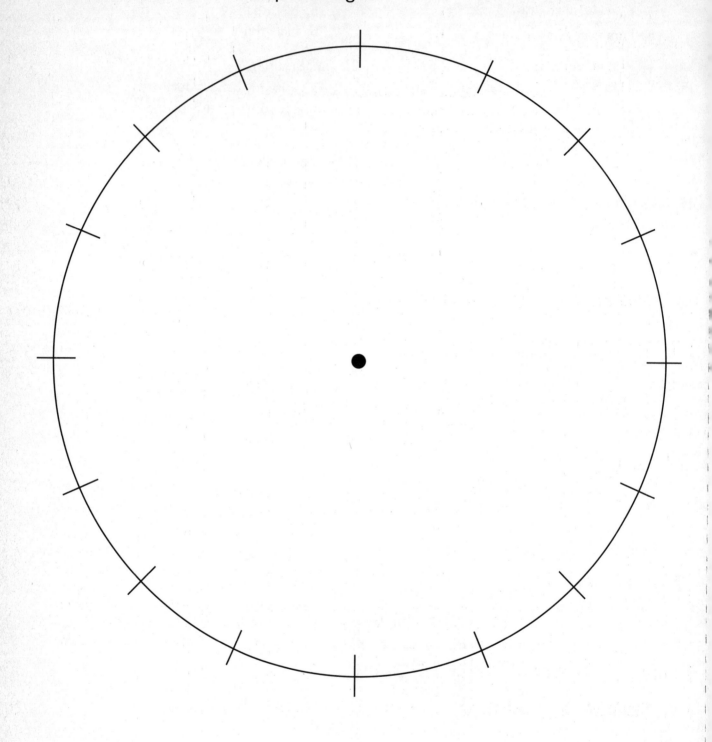

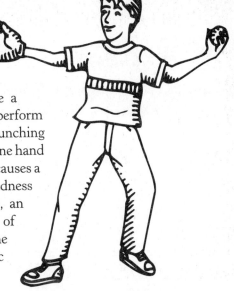

Are You Handy?

Step One }
MAKE AN OBSERVATION.
Do you prefer to do certain tasks with a certain side of your body? Most people have a dominant hand they use when they write and perform other tasks such as eating, dialing a phone, or punching numbers into a calculator. The tendency to use one hand is known as *handedness*. Scientists wonder what causes a person to be left- or right-handed. Does handedness run in families? Is handedness a genetic trait, an example of learned behavior, or a combination of both? Is handedness related to the side of the body preferred to perform other kinesthetic tasks, such as kicking a ball?

Step Two }
STATE THE PROBLEM AND POSE IT AS A RESEARCH QUESTION.
Conduct a study to determine if handedness and being a member of the same family influences/determines the side of the body an individual prefers for performing various kinesthetic tasks such as writing, putting on a shoe, or looking through a tube.

> What is the effect you observe?

> What is the possible cause of the effect?

> How can it be posed as a research question?

Step Three }
CONDUCT YOUR RESEARCH.
Research the terms *handedness, genetic traits, learned behavior,* and *kinesthetic tasks* to find out what they are and how they are connected. Then write a summary that communicates your findings.

Step Four }
FORMULATE A HYPOTHESIS.
Identify the independent variable (the part of the experiment that is different) and the dependent variable (the part of the experiment that is affected by what is different). Write your hypothesis as a positive statement that predicts a connection between handedness and the preferred side for other kinesthetic tasks in a group of genetically related individuals. Or write a negative statement that predicts no connection between handedness and the side preferred for other tasks.

Step Five }
DESIGN AND CONDUCT YOUR EXPERIMENT.
A. Identify variables you will keep the same during the experiment. Consider how your group is demographically the same. Consider using the same test or method of evaluation, and test under the same conditions.

0-7696-3429-X *Science Fair Projects: Volume 2*

B. Materials: study group composed of 20 members of the same family (parents, children, aunts, uncles, cousins, grandparents, etc.), 20 consent forms, 2 copies kinesthetic-task survey form, and data table

C. Procedure

1. Select 20 members of the same family to survey. Ask them to sign consent forms (p. 27).

2. Arrange a time for each family member to take the kinesthetic survey on page 28.

3. Record the results for each body part tested in the survey.

4. When data has been collected from all 20 participants, use tables 2.4 and 2.5 below to find the total number and percentage of participants who preferred each side.

D. Collect data.

Table 2.4   Kinesthetic results

Part tested	Left preference tallies	Right preference tallies	Total left	Total right
Hand				
Arm				
Eye				
Foot/leg				

Use this formula to convert the numbers from table 2.4 to percentages in table 2.5.

$$(n \div 20) \times 100,$$

in which n = number of people with a preference ÷ total number of participants (20). *(Round your answer to the nearest whole number.)*

Table 2.5   Calculate percentages

Results	Hand	Arm	Eye	Foot/leg
Number with right preference				
÷ total number of people surveyed				
x 100 = percentage with right preference				
Number with left preference				
÷ total number of people surveyed				
x 100 = percentage with left preference				

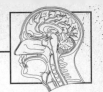

Step Six } **COMMUNICATE YOUR DATA IN AN APPROPRIATE MANNER.**
Use a double bar graph to communicate the results of your survey. To construct a double bar graph, use two colors—one to communicate the percentage of people with a right-side preference, and another to communicate the percentage of people with a left-side preference. Include a key to show which color communicates which side. Use the graph outline on page 29.

Step Seven } **ANALYZE THE RESULTS TO DRAW A CONCLUSION.** Write a conclusion statement that summarizes your findings, states whether or not your hypothesis was correct, and tells which side was preferred. If there is a connection between the hand preference and the side of the body preferred for other kinesthetic tasks among the members of the family surveyed, then the numbers for that side will be very similar. If there is no connection, then the numbers will be very different.

Step Eight } **EXPLAIN YOUR FINDINGS WITH AN INFERENCE.** Logically explain why your data turned out the way it did. Infer if you think this is due to a genetic link, a learned behavior, or a combination of both.

Alternatives and extensions

1. Choose a different demographic group, such as a group of 30 members of the same age group, and conduct the study to determine what the dominant side and/or handedness is for a particular age group.

2. Choose different-aged subjects that are not related to each other to determine if age has an effect on side preference and handedness.

3. Choose a different family group for the test. See if different families produce similar percentages of handedness.

- -

CONSENT: Are You Handy?

I consent to take part in a study to determine if there is a connection between the hand I prefer to use for writing and the side of my body that I use for other kinesthetic tasks. I understand that the results of my survey will be used as data in a science fair project. I also understand that my name will not be used or published.

Printed name of participant _____

Signature_____ Date _____

Published by Milestone. Copyright protected.

Kinesthetic Survey

Task	Left side	Right side
Hand		
Hand used to write your name on the paper		
Thumb on top when your hands are clasped		
Hand used to pour water into a cup		
Hand used to lift a cup to drink water		
Hand used to take the cap off of the toothpaste		
Hand used to put toothpaste on a toothbrush		
Hand used to brush your teeth		
Hand used to put numbers into a calculator		
Hand used to hold telephone to your ear		
Hand used to open a book		
Hand that is larger when you put your hands together		
Total: Add the marks in each column for this section.		
Arm		
Arm that is put into shirt first		
Arm that is washed first when taking a shower or bath		
Arm used to wave to someone		
Arm used to support a stack of books		
Arm used to push a basketball when shooting a basket		
Arm used to throw a ball		
Arm that is longer when measured		
Total: Add the marks in each column for this section.		
Eye		
Close one eye and read a book—Which eye is open?		
Eye used to look through an empty paper towel tube		
Eye used to look at a book through a hand lens		
Eye used to wink		
Eye that is more open when you squint		
Total: Add the marks in each column for this section.		
Foot/Leg		
First foot you put a shoe on		
Leg that goes in your pants first		
Leg on top when your legs are crossed		
Foot on top when your feet are crossed		
Foot used to kick a ball		
Foot put first when taking a step		
Foot that is longer when measured		
Foot placed on stair first		
Leg that is longer when measured		
Total: Add the marks in each column for this section.		

0-7696-3429-X *Science Fair Projects: Volume 2*

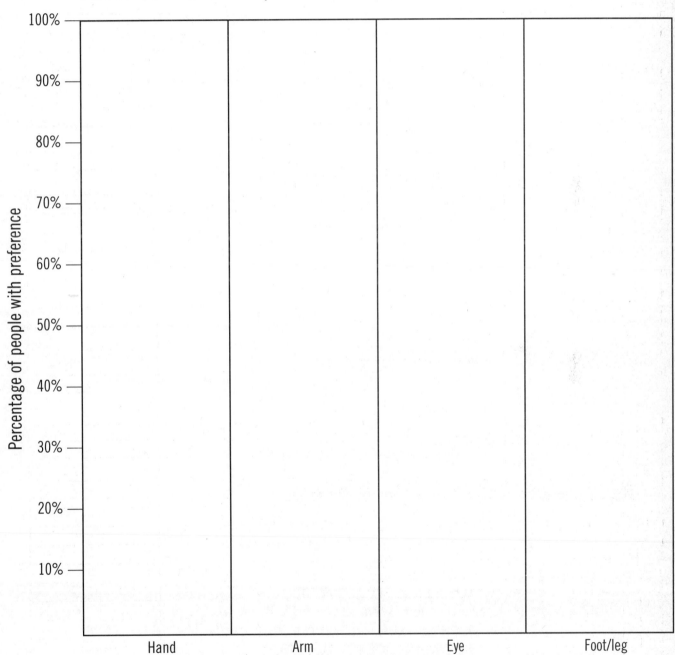

Handedness and side preferences for kinesthetic tasks

Percentage of people with preference

100%

90%

80%

70%

60%

50%

40%

30%

20%

10%

Hand   Arm   Eye   Foot/leg

Part of body tested

Can You Read in Color?

Step One } **MAKE AN OBSERVATION.** Have you ever noticed that it is very difficult to perform some tasks at the same time, such as singing a song while trying to do your math homework? Some people think this is because different parts of the brain are better at different tasks. They say most people rely more heavily on one hemisphere of the brain to process information. This tendency is known as brain dominance. Human brains have two hemispheres—the left and the right. These people hypothesize that the right hemisphere processes nonverbal, concrete, and spatial information, while the left hemisphere processes verbal, abstract, and analytical information. Tasks such as reading or doing math problems use the left hemisphere, while tasks such as singing or recognizing colors use the creative tendencies of the right hemisphere.

Step Two } **STATE THE PROBLEM AND POSE IT AS A RESEARCH QUESTION.** Scientists wonder how the rate that a simple task is performed is affected when both hemispheres work in mental competition. In this investigation, you will be conducting a demographic study using a poster of the names of colors. The color words will be in a different color than the name of the color. Your task is to find out how the time it takes to read the uncolored words (thought to be a single-hemisphere task) is related to the time it takes to read the words in different colors (thought to require mental competition between the two hemispheres).

> What is the effect you observe?

> What is the possible cause of the effect?

> How can it be posed as a research question?

Step Three } **CONDUCT YOUR RESEARCH.** Investigate the terms *cognition, demographic study, brain dominance, left-hemisphere characteristics, right-hemisphere characteristics,* and *lateral thinking.* Also investigate which hemisphere is considered responsible for learning to read language and which hemisphere is considered responsible for recognizing colors. Write a summary that explains your findings.

Step Four } **FORMULATE A HYPOTHESIS.** Identify the independent variable that will be changed in your experiment. Identify the dependent variable that is affected by what you change. Write a testable hypothesis that predicts the relationship between the independent and dependent variables. Your hypothesis should predict a relationship or no relationship between the time it takes a reader to read a set of words based solely on word recognition and the time it takes the reader to read the same set of words against color recognition.

(30)

Step Five } DESIGN AND CONDUCT YOUR EXPERIMENT.

A. Identify the variables you will keep the same during the experiment. Consider using the same age group for your study, the same color sheets, the same timing method, and the same time of day.

B. Materials: 2 color-words posters copied from page 35, a group of 20 participants, consent form on page 34, data table (p. 32), and a stopwatch

C. Procedure

1. Make two copies of the color-words poster.

2. On one poster, color each word a different color than the color it names.

3. Select your study group, making sure that your subjects are the same age.

4. Have each subject fill out and sign a consent form.

5. Have the participant begin by reading the uncolored words aloud. Record in the data table the amount of time it takes to read the entire poster. (Keep track of any errors and record this information in the table as well.)

6. Have the participant repeat step 5. Average the two times together.

7. Instruct the participant to read the words on the color poster. Record in the data table the amount of time it takes to read the entire poster. (Keep track of any errors and record this information as well.)

8. Have the participant repeat step 7. Average the two times together.

9. Follow steps 5–8 for the remaining nineteen participants.

10. Find the average amount of time it took all of the participants to read the uncolored words by adding together all of the participants' average times and then dividing by 20. Record the average in the table.

11. Find the average amount of time it took all of the participants to read the colored words by adding all the average times together and then dividing the total by 20. Record this average in the table.

D. Collect Data. Use the table on page 32 to record times and errors of poster-reading trials (20 participants with two trials each).

Table 2.6

Participant and task	Trial 1 (time in secs.)	Trial 2 (time in secs.)	Total time	÷ 2	Average time	Number of Errors	
						Trial 1	Trial 2
1. Uncolored				÷ 2			
1. Colored				÷ 2			
2. Uncolored				÷ 2			
2. Colored				÷ 2			
3. Uncolored				÷ 2			
3. Colored				÷ 2			
4. Uncolored				÷ 2			
4. Colored				÷ 2			
5. Uncolored				÷ 2			
5. Colored				÷ 2			
6. Uncolored				÷ 2			
6. Colored				÷ 2			
7. Uncolored				÷ 2			
7. Colored				÷ 2			
8. Uncolored				÷ 2			
8. Colored				÷ 2			
9. Uncolored				÷ 2			
9. Colored				÷ 2			
10. Uncolored				÷ 2			
10. Colored				÷ 2			
11. Uncolored				÷ 2			
11. Colored				÷ 2			
12. Uncolored				÷ 2			
12. Colored				÷ 2			
13. Uncolored				÷ 2			
13. Colored				÷ 2			
14. Uncolored				÷ 2			
14. Colored				÷ 2			
15. Uncolored				÷ 2			
15. Colored				÷ 2			
16. Uncolored				÷ 2			
16. Colored				÷ 2			
17. Uncolored				÷ 2			
17. Colored				÷ 2			
18. Uncolored				÷ 2			
18. Colored				÷ 2			
19. Uncolored				÷ 2			
19. Colored				÷ 2			
20. Uncolored				÷ 2			
20. Colored				÷ 2			
Avg. Uncolored				÷ 2			
Avg. Colored				÷ 2			

0-7696-3429-X *Science Fair Projects: Volume 2*

Step Six } **COMMUNICATE YOUR DATA IN AN APPROPRIATE MANNER.** Because you are comparing the amount of time it took each participant to read the uncolored and colored words, the best tool to show your results is a double bar graph (see p. 34). Label the *x*-axis "Participant's number." Number it from 1–20, skipping a line between each number. Label the *y*-axis "Time to perform task (seconds)." Decide how you will number the axis by looking at the range of your data. You will want to use two colors to construct two bars for each participant—one color for average time to read uncolored words and one for average time to read colored words. Include a key to indicate what the colors of the bars represent. Finally, add a title to your graph.

Step Seven } **ANALYZE YOUR DATA AND DRAW A CONCLUSION.** Based on your data, write a summary that expresses whether or not your hypothesis was correct. Also explain which tasks took the least and most time and which tasks had the fewest or most errors.

Step Eight } **EXPLAIN YOUR FINDINGS WITH AN INFERENCE.** Logically explain why the results turned out the way they did based on your research.

Alternatives and extensions

1. Tabulate the information you collected in the experiment on number of errors. Use the same methods to average them. How do these numbers correlate to the rest of your data?

2. Perform the same study using a demographic group made up of different-aged participants to determine if age has an affect on ability to perform a multihemisphere task.

Consent: Reading in Color

I consent to take part in a study to determine if the time it takes to read uncolored words is the same amount of time it takes to read colored words. I understand that the results of my survey will be used as data in a science fair project. I also understand that my name will not be used or published.

Printed name of participant _____

Signature _____ Date _____

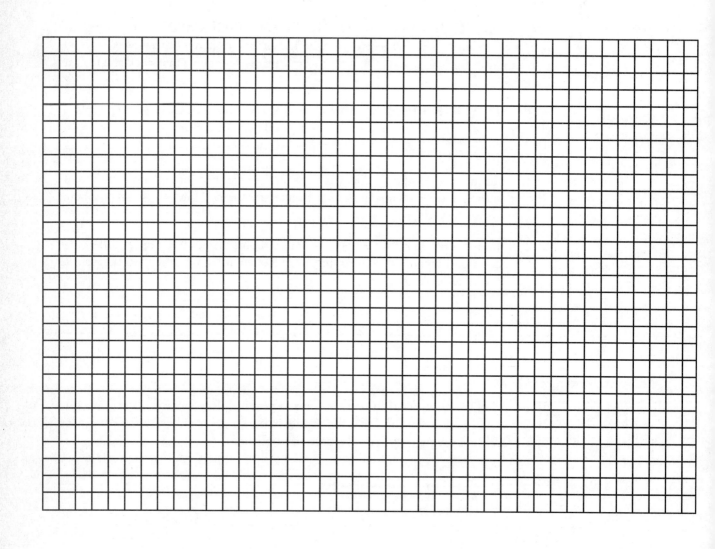

0-7696-3429-X *Science Fair Projects: Volume 2*

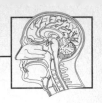

RED BLUE PINK
WHITE GREEN
ORANGE BLACK
INDIGO YELLOW
PURPLE BROWN
BLACK RED PINK
PURPLE ORANGE
YELLOW BLUE
WHITE INDIGO

0-7696-3429-X *Science Fair Projects: Volume 2*

Tasting Colors

Step One } **MAKE AN OBSERVATION.** Have you noticed that color plays an important role in the foods you select and what flavors you expect to taste? Scientists define this tendency to associate a specific color with a specific taste as a *stimulus response*. The color is a stimulus we have learned to respond to in a specific way. The Egyptians were the first to experiment with this concept in 1500 B.C., when they added color to prepared candies to make them more appealing. Food engineers today use synthetic and natural dyes to make food look more appealing.

Step Two } **STATE THE PROBLEM AND POSE IT AS A RESEARCH QUESTION.** Identify the effect of color on how people identify the flavors of foods. You will conduct an investigation to determine if subjects respond to the stimulus of color.

> What is the effect you observe?

> What is the possible cause of the effect?

> How can it be posed as a research question?

Step Three } **CONDUCT YOUR RESEARCH.** Investigate the terms *behavioral conditioning, demographic study, stimulus,* and *response.* Also investigate what types of human behavior result from behavioral conditioning. Write a summary that communicates what you find out.

Step Four } **FORMULATE A HYPOTHESIS.** Identify the independent variable you will change in your experiment. Identify the dependent variable that is affected by what you change. Write a testable hypothesis that predicts the relationship between the independent and dependent variables. Your hypothesis may be a positive statement that predicts a direct relationship between the color of the food and the flavor tasted, indicating a conditioned stimulus response. Or your hypothesis may be a negative statement that predicts no relationship between color and taste, indicating no conditioned stimulus response.

Step Five } **DESIGN AND CONDUCT YOUR EXPERIMENT.**

A. Identify the variables you will keep the same during the experiment. Consider using the same age group for your study, the same colors of gelatin, the same flavoring, and the same testing process

B. Materials: 12 packets of unflavored gelatin; red, yellow, green, and blue food coloring; cherry, lemon, and orange flavor extracts; pipettes; sugar; a saucepan; water; 6 square 8-inch pans; waxed paper; a measuring cup; 30 participants; 30 copies of table 2.7 (p. 37); 30 small paper plates; saltine crackers; drinking water, and 30 consent forms (p. 40)

C. Procedure

1. Select 30 participants the same age. Have each participant fill out and sign a consent form.

2. Prepare your gelatin samples according to the following directions.

   a. Heat 1 cup water in a small saucepan until it boils.

   b. Open 2 packets of unflavored gelatin and pour them into a mixing bowl.

   c. Add the boiling water to the gelatin and stir until it dissolves.

   d. Add 1/3 cup of sugar and stir until the sugar dissolves.

   e. Add 3 to 4 drops of red food coloring to 1 cup of cold water. Add to sugar water and stir.

   f. Use a pipette to add 1/10 ml each of cherry, lemon, and orange extracts. Stir to mix.

   g. Line a baking pan with waxed paper and pour the gelatin mixture into the pan.

   h. Allow the gelatin to set in the refrigerator and then cut it in 30 cubes.

   i. Repeat the steps to make orange, yellow, green, purple, and blue gelatin squares. Add the same amounts of all the flavor extracts to all the samples.

3. If possible, try to test all of the participants around the same time to ensure the freshness of your samples. When testing, give each participant a sample of each color of gelatin on a plate, a pencil, and a copy of the individual table (below).

4. Give each participant a copy of table 2.7 (below). Instruct the participants to write what they expect each color gelatin to taste like. Then ask them to taste each sample and write the flavor they taste.

5. Provide water and saltine crackers to clean the participants' palates between tastings.

6. Use table 2.8 (p. 38) to tabulate your results. Write in the different flavors that were predicted for each gelatin sample. Use tally marks to indicate how many participants predicted each flavor.

7. Use table 2.9 (p. 38) to tabulate your results. Write the different flavors tasted for each gelatin sample. Use tally marks to indicate how many participants tasted each flavor.

D. Collect data.

Table 2.7   Taste test

Gelatin color	Flavor I expect	Flavor I taste
Red		
Orange		
Green		
Yellow		
Purple		
Blue		

Table 2.8　Predicting flavors

Red gelatin			
Predicted flavors			
No. of participants			
Orange gelatin			
Predicted flavors			
No. of participants			
Green gelatin			
Predicted flavors			
No. of participants			
Yellow gelatin			
Predicted flavors			
No. of participants			
Purple gelatin			
Predicted flavors			
No. of participants			
Blue gelatin			
Predicted flavors			
No. of participants			

Table 2.9　Tasting flavors

Red gelatin			
Tasted flavors			
No. of participants			
Orange gelatin			
Tasted flavors			
No. of participants			
Green gelatin			
Tasted flavors			
No. of participants			
Yellow gelatin			
Tasted flavors			
No. of participants			
Purple gelatin			
Tasted flavors			
No. of participants			
Blue gelatin			
Tasted flavors			
No. of participants			

0-7696-3429-X *Science Fair Projects: Volume 2*

Step Six } **COMMUNICATE YOUR DATA IN AN APPROPRIATE MANNER.** Because you are comparing two different sets of data in this investigation, the best tool is a double bar graph (see p. 40). Create a double bar graph for each color gelatin to compare flavors predicted and tasted. Label the *x*-axis "Flavor," and write in the different flavors. Label the *y*-axis "Number of participants." Number this axis by twos. Use colored pencils to indicate predicted and tasted flavors. Include a key. Use the graph outline on page 40 to create six graphs—one for each color gelatin.

Step Seven } **ANALYZE YOUR DATA AND DRAW A CONCLUSION.** Based on your data, write a summary that expresses whether or not there is a conditioned stimulus response between the color of gelatin and its flavor. If a conditioned stimulus response exists, then you should find that the majority of your participants tasted the same flavor they predicted. You may also find that some colors, such as red or orange, indicate conditioning while other colors, such as blue, do not.

Step Eight } **EXPLAIN YOUR FINDINGS WITH AN INFERENCE.** Logically explain why the results turned out the way that they did based on your research.

Alternatives and extensions

1. Scientists conduct color studies to find out how people respond to specific colors. Scientific findings influence the colors designers and architects use in public buildings, as well as the colors engineers use for headlights and streetlights. Conduct your own study to determine if 30 participants the same age are conditioned to exhibit a specific emotion in response to a particular color by asking how the colors red, blue, green, yellow, and brown make them feel.

2. The makers of M&M's rely on demographic studies similar to this one to determine the ratio of colors to put in their colorful candy mix. Past results indicate that most participants preferred brown chocolate candies. Conduct a study by surveying a group of 30 participants the same age. Ask which color of M&M's they like best to determine whether brown is still the preferred color. Then visit the M&M's Web site to find the current ratio of colors in a bag of M&M 's.

M&M's is a registered trademark of Mars, Inc.

Consent: Tasting Colors

I consent to take part in a study to determine if color influences flavors I taste. I understand that the results of my taste test will be used as data in a science fair project. I also understand that my name will not be used or published.

Printed name of participant _____

Signature _____ Date _____

Does color predict taste?

Number of participants

Flavors

Key

Predicted flavor

Tasted flavor

Do You Measure Up?

Step One }

MAKE AN OBSERVATION. Do you wonder how forensic scientists and anthropologists can tell how tall a person was by examining the person's bones? With 206 bones forming the human skeleton, it's not surprising that scientists can gain a lot of information by studying bones. Forensic scientists and anthropologists can estimate the heights, ages, and builds of deceased animals and people by looking for relationships and patterns in the skeletal systems of living animals and people. The length of certain bones helps scientists determine the height of an individual by using a mathematical formula. Discernable differences between the bones of males and females allows scientists to identify the sex of skeletal remains. Bones are more than just a framework to hold a body upright and protect its organs. Bones also provide scientists with valuable information that can be used to reconstruct the past.

Step Two }

STATE THE PROBLEM AND POSE IT AS A RESEARCH QUESTION. Determine if the formulas used by anthropologists and forensic scientists to infer the height of an individual based on her or his skeletal remains are valid. You will conduct a demographic study with some of your classmates as subjects to compare actual heights with calculated heights.

> What is the effect you observe?

> What is the possible cause of the effect?

> How can it be posed as a research question?

Step Three }

CONDUCT YOUR RESEARCH. Investigate what anthropologists and forensic scientists do and investigate how they look for relationships and patterns in living things to draw conclusions about deceased animals and people. Write a summary of your findings to include in your presentation.

Step Four }

FORMULATE A HYPOTHESIS. Identify the independent variable that changes in your experiment. Identify the dependent variable that is affected by what you change. Write a testable hypothesis that predicts the relationship between the independent and dependent variables. Your hypothesis may predict that all of the formulas you test provide the same level of accuracy, you may predict that one formula is more accurate than the others, or you may predict that none of the formulas provide an accurate calculation.

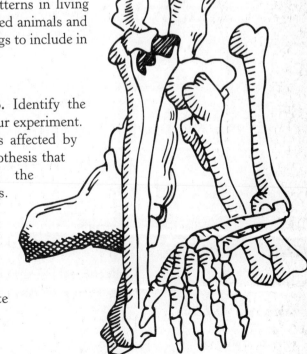

Step Five } DESIGN AND CONDUCT YOUR EXPERIMENT.

Identify the variables you will keep the same during the experiment. Consider using subjects who are about the same age, using the same measuring tools for all of your measurements, and using the same method to obtain the measurements.

Materials: A group of 15 males and 15 females about the same age, 30 consent forms, a metric measuring tape, and a calculator

Procedure

1. Select your demographic group and have each participant fill out and sign a consent form.

2. Determine where the radius, humerus, and tibia are located using the skeleton diagram on page 48. Decide what method you will use to make your measurements. Write the procedure you will use to measure the length of each bone. Make all of your measurements in centimeters.

3. Determine how you will measure each subject's height and write your procedure for that.

4. Follow your procedures in steps 2 and 3 to measure each participant. Record your measurements in the correct data tables (pp. 43–45).

5. Use the formulas accompanying each table to calculate each subject's height based on the length of the specified bone.

6. Find the difference between the calculated height and the measured height. Record it in the appropriate data table.

7. Use this formula to calculate the percentage of error between the two measurements.

$$(y \div x) \times 100,$$

in which y = the difference between the calculated height and the measured height and x = the measured height.

8. Complete the tables for all 30 subjects.

9. Find the average percentage of error for the data in each table by adding them and dividing by 15 (the number of participants).

10. Add the 3 average percents of error for the male data and divide by 3 to find the percentage of error. Repeat to find the percentage of error for the female data. Record these numbers to use in your graph.

Collect data. Use the tables on pages 43–45 to record your statistics and calculations.

Published by Milestone. Copyright protected.

0-7696-3429-X *Science Fair Projects: Volume 2*

Table 2.10 Male heights and tibia lengths

Formula: Height = 32.2 cm + (2.4 x length of tibia in cm)

Participant	Tibia length (cm)	x 2.4	+ 32.2 cm	= Calculated height (cm)	Measured height x (cm)	Diff. in height y (cm)	% of error $(y \div x)$ x 100
1			+ 32.2 cm				
2			+ 32.2 cm				
3			+ 32.2 cm				
4			+ 32.2 cm				
5			+ 32.2 cm				
6			+ 32.2 cm				
7			+ 32.2 cm				
8			+ 32.2 cm				
9			+ 32.2 cm				
10			+ 32.2 cm				
11			+ 32.2 cm				
12			+ 32.2 cm				
13			+ 32.2 cm				
14			+ 32.2 cm				
15			+ 32.2 cm				

Average percent of error_____

Table 2.11 Male heights and humerus lengths

Formula: Height = 29.0 cm + (3.0 x length of humerus in cm)

Participant	Humerus length (cm)	x 3.0	+ 29.0 cm	= Calculated height (cm)	Measured height x (cm)	Diff. in height y (cm)	% of error $(y \div x)$ x 100
1			+ 29.0 cm				
2			+ 29.0 cm				
3			+ 29.0 cm				
4			+ 29.0 cm				
5			+ 29.0 cm				
6			+ 29.0 cm				
7			+ 29.0 cm				
8			+ 29.0 cm				
9			+ 29.0 cm				
10			+ 29.0 cm				
11			+ 29.0 cm				
12			+ 29.0cm				
13			+ 29.0 cm				
14			+ 29.0 cm				
15			+ 29.0 cm				

Average percent of error_____

   0-7696-3429-X *Science Fair Projects: Volume 2*

Table 2.12   Male heights and radius lengths

Formula: Height = 31.7 cm + (3.7 x length of radius in cm)

Participant	Radius length (cm)	x 3.7	+ 31.7 cm	= Calculated height (cm)	Measured height x (cm)	Diff. in height y (cm)	% of error $(y \div x) \times 100$
1			+ 31.7 cm				
2			+ 31.7 cm				
3			+ 31.7 cm				
4			+ 31.7 cm				
5			+ 31.7 cm				
6			+ 31.7 cm				
7			+ 31.7 cm				
8			+ 31.7 cm				
9			+ 31.7 cm				
10			+ 31.7 cm				
11			+ 31.7 cm				
12			+ 31.7 cm				
13			+ 31.7 cm				
14			+ 31.7 cm				
15			+ 31.7 cm				

Average percent of error _____

Table 2.13   Female heights and tibia lengths

Formula: Height = 28.6 cm + (2.5 x tibia length in cm)

Participant	Tibia length (cm)	x 2.5	+ 28.6 cm	= Calculated height (cm)	Measured height x (cm)	Diff. in height y (cm)	% of error $(y \div x) \times 100$
1			+ 28.6 cm				
2			+ 28.6 cm				
3			+ 28.6 cm				
4			+ 28.6 cm				
5			+ 28.6 cm				
6			+ 28.6 cm				
7			+ 28.6 cm				
8			+ 28.6 cm				
9			+ 28.6 cm				
10			+ 28.6 cm				
11			+ 28.6 cm				
12			+ 28.6 cm				
13			+ 28.6 cm				
14			+ 28.6 cm				
15			+ 28.6 cm				

Average percent of error _____

0-7696-3429-X *Science Fair Projects: Volume 2*

Table 2.14 Female heights and humerus lengths

Formula: Height = 25.6 cm + (3.1 x length of humerus in cm)

Participant	Humerus length (cm)	x 3.1	+ 25.6 cm	= Calculated height (cm)	Measured height x (cm)	Diff. in height y (cm)	% of error $(y \div x)$ x 100
1			+ 25.6 cm				
2			+ 25.6 cm				
3			+ 25.6 cm				
4			+ 25.6 cm				
5			+ 25.6 cm				
6			+ 25.6 cm				
7			+ 25.6 cm				
8			+ 25.6 cm				
9			+ 25.6 cm				
10			+ 25.6 cm				
11			+ 25.6 cm				
12			+ 25.6 cm				
13			+ 25.6 cm				
14			+ 25.6 cm				
15			+ 25.6 cm				

Average percent of error _____

Table 2.15 Female heights and radius lengths

Formula: Height = 28.9 cm + (3.9 x length of radius in cm)

Participant	Radius Length (cm)	X 3.9 =	+ 28.9 cm	= Calc. Height (cm)	Measured x Height (cm)	Diff. in y Height (cm)	% of Error $(y \div x)$ x 100
1			+ 28.9 cm				
2			+ 28.9 cm				
3			+ 28.9 cm				
4			+ 28.9 cm				
5			+ 28.9 cm				
6			+ 28.9 cm				
7			+ 28.9 cm				
8			+ 28.9 cm				
9			+ 28.9 cm				
10			+ 28.9 cm				
11			+ 28.9 cm				
12			+ 28.9 cm				
13			+ 28.9 cm				
14			+ 28.9 cm				
15			+ 28.9 cm				

Average percent of error _____

0-7696-3429-X *Science Fair Projects: Volume 2*

Step Six } **COMMUNICATE YOUR DATA IN AN APPROPRIATE MANNER.** Because you are comparing the percent of error for males and for females for three formulas, the best tool is a double bar graph. Label the *x*-axis "Bone used for calculation." Identify the bones along this axis. Because you have data for males and for females, each bone requires two bars. The *y*-axis should be labeled "Average percent of error." Determine how to number the *y*-axis by looking at the range of your data from the lowest to the highest value. Use one color to show the data for males and another color to show the data for females. Provide a key and add a title to your graph.

Step Seven } **ANALYZE YOUR DATA TO DRAW CONCLUSIONS.** Based on your data, write a conclusion that summarizes your findings, states whether or not your hypothesis was correct, and identifies which bone formula or gender's data was least and most accurate. This can be determined by looking for the calculations that resulted in the lowest and highest percentages of error.

Step Eight } **EXPLAIN YOUR FINDINGS WITH AN INFERENCE.** Logically explain why the results of your experiment came out the way they did, based on your research.

Alternatives and extensions

1. Use the same procedure to find out if an individual's age effects the accuracy of the calculated height based on a forensic bone length formula by using a demographic group made up of people in different age groups. You may wish to choose either males or females in this investigation.

2. Research what other proportional relationships are believed to exist between the bones of the human skeleton. Use the same type of procedure to conduct a study to determine the validity of the relationship.

- -

Consent: Do You Measure Up?

I consent to take part in a study to determine how accurate different bone measurements are at calculating my actual height. I understand that the results of my survey will be used as data in a science fair project. I also understand that my name will not be used or published.

Printed name of participant _____

Signature_____ Date _____

Published by Milestone. Copyright protected.

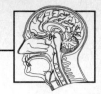

Key

Male ☐

Female ☐

Average percent of error

Tibia   Humerus   Radius

Bone used for calculation

0-7696-3429-X *Science Fair Projects: Volume 2*

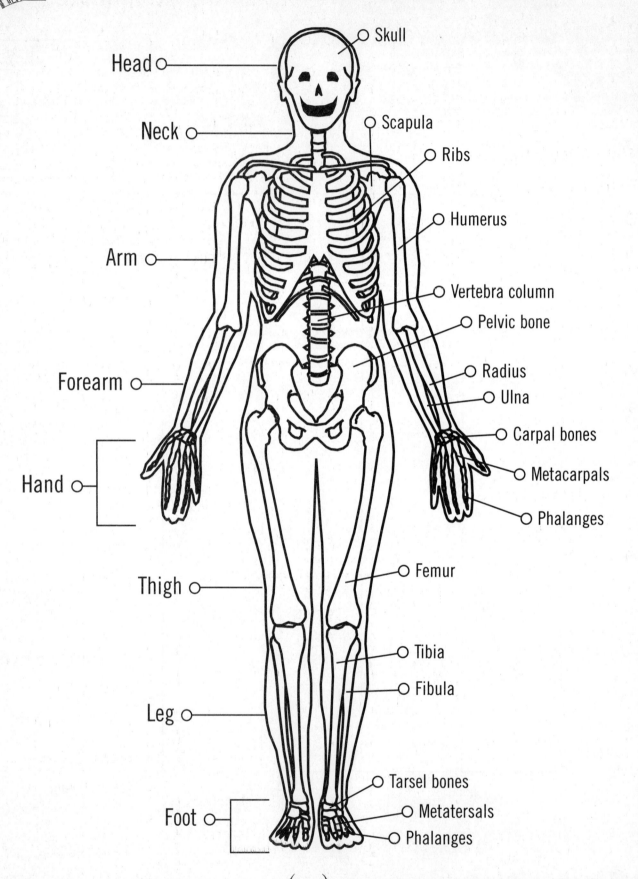

Head o
Skull
Neck o
Scapula
Ribs
Humerus
Arm o
Vertebra column
Pelvic bone
Forearm o
Radius
Ulna
Carpal bones
Hand o
Metacarpals
Phalanges
Thigh o
Femur
Tibia
Fibula
Leg o
Tarsel bones
Foot o
Metatersals
Phalanges

It's Not Raining Rain, You Know?

Step One } **MAKE AN OBSERVATION.** Have you ever noticed that sidewalks in some places seem to crumble faster than sidewalks in other places? Scientists have discovered that this is due to acid rain. Acid rain is precipitation that is more acidic than normal. All precipitation is slightly acidic because clean, or unpolluted, rain has a slightly acidic pH of 5.6. The carbon dioxide and water in the air react together to form carbonic acid, a weak acid. By measuring the pH of the rain falling in different places, scientists have found that the acidity level of the rain falling in industrialized regions has increased. The extra acidity in acid rain comes from the reaction with air pollutants. The main sources of these pollutants are emissions from power plants, factories, vehicles, and homes where fossil fuels are burnt.

Step Two } **STATE THE PROBLEM AND POSE IT AS A RESEARCH QUESTION.** Scientists have questioned what effect acid rain with different pH levels has on building materials, particularly those containing limestone, a common ingredient in concrete. In this investigation, you will use solutions with different acidities to find out what effect they have on samples of limestone.

> What is the effect you observe?

> What is the possible cause of the effect?

> How can it be posed as a research question?

Step Three } **CONDUCT YOUR RESEARCH.** Investigate the terms *pH, indicators, acid rain, pollution, pollutants,* and *deterioration.* Also, research to find out what building materials contain limestone as a key ingredient. Write a summary that communicates your findings.

Step Four } **FORMULATE A HYPOTHESIS.** Identify the independent variable you will change in your experiment. Identify the dependent variable that will be affected by what you change. Write a testable hypothesis that predicts the relationship between the independent and dependent variables. Your hypothesis may either be a positive statement—that there is a connection between the acidity level and the deterioration of limestone—or a negative statement—that there is not a connection between the two variables.

Step Five } **DESIGN AND CONDUCT YOUR EXPERIMENT:**

A. Identify the variables you will keep the same during the experiment. Consider using the same type of limestone, same size samples, the same testing place, the same amount of time, the same method to test the samples.

B. Materials: 16 samples of limestone rock about the same size (often sold as driveway or road gravel, available at your local concrete distributor), 15 portion cups or other shallow containers, a sunny place, paper towels, red cabbage juice indicator strips (recipe on p. 50), vinegar, fresh lemon juice, household ammonia, distilled water, club soda, red cabbage indicator scale (p. 51), and safety goggles

0-7696-3429-X *Science Fair Projects: Volume 2*

C. Procedure

1. Wash your rock samples in warm water and allow them to thoroughly dry on paper towels.

2. Prepare your red cabbage indicator strips and set them aside.

    a. Cut 1/2 a head of red cabbage into small pieces.

    b. Place the cut cabbage in a blender and completely cover with hot water.

    c. Blend on high for 3–5 minutes, until the water turns purple and the cabbage turns to pulp.

    d. Strain the mixture through a colander lined with a coffee filter.

    e. Strain the mixture a second time to ensure that all of the cabbage pulp is removed.

    f. Dip several clean coffee filters in the strained cabbage juice and set them on a piece of wax paper to dry.

    g. Cut the dry coffee filters into strips.

3. Use your dry indicator strips to test the pH of the distilled water, club soda, vinegar, lemon juice, and ammonia by dipping a strip into each liquid to see what color the strip turns.

4. Record your observations in table 3.1 (p. 51). Use table 3.2 (p. 51) to find the pH value of each solution. Record the values in table 3.1.

5. Label 15 containers as follows:

    Label 3 containers Distilled Water. These are your control.

    Label 3 containers for each: Club Soda, Vinegar, Lemon Juice, and Ammonia.

CAUTION: Wear safety goggles when using the liquids.

6. Place the dry limestone samples in the labeled containers. Add the appropriate solution to each container to almost completely cover the sample.

7. Observe the limestone when you add the solution to each container. Record your observations in the table on page 53.

8. Place all of your samples in a sunny place where they will not be disturbed for several days. Record observations each day.

9. On day 7, label 5 sheets of paper towel to match the labels on your containers.

10. Using tongs, carefully remove the limestone samples from the containers and put them on the corresponding paper towels.

11. Allow the samples to dry. Examine each and record your final observations in the table on page 53.

D. Collect data.

Table 3.1   What's the pH?

Solution	Indicator color	pH value from table
Distilled water		
Club soda		
Vinegar		
Fresh lemon juice		
Ammonia		

Table 3.2   Red cabbage pH scale

Type of solution	pH	Indicator color
Strong acid	1	Orange
	2	Orange-red
	3	Red
	4	Bright pink
	5	Magenta
Weak acid	6	Purplish-pink
Neutral	7	Purple
Weak base	8	Blue
	9	Turquoise
	10	Blue-green
	11	Green-blue
	12	Green
	13	Yellow-green
Strong base	14	Yellow

Step Six } **COMMUNICATE YOUR DATA IN AN APPROPRIATE MANNER.** Because the observations made in this experiment were qualitative, meaning that you used your senses to collect data, you should include your observation table in your presentation. Also include the table that shows the pH of each solution used.

Step Seven } **ANALYZE YOUR DATA TO DRAW CONCLUSIONS.** Based on your data, write a conclusion that summarizes your findings, states whether or not your hypothesis was correct, and identifies ways your data could be used to help make building decisions.

Step Eight } **EXPLAIN YOUR FINDINGS WITH AN INFERENCE.** Logically explain why the results of your experiment came out the way they did, based on your research.

Alternatives and extensions

1. Use the solutions from this investigation to determine how pH level affects plant growth. Use 15 identical potted plants. "Water" each plant with one of the solutions. Observe the plants over a period of two weeks and record your observations. Plants should be planted in the same area to ensure that the soil is the same and that they receive the same amount of sunlight (or keep in pots placed in the same area). Create a table that shows the plant growth by measuring the plants each day and recording the results in your observation table.

2. Collect rain samples from different areas in your neighborhood and determine the pH level of the samples. Use clean containers and put them in places they will not be disturbed. Consider testing areas such as under a roof where the rain runs down, under a tree branch, away from obstacles, and so on.

Observing limestone in solutions with different pH values

Day	Samples in ammonia	Samples in fresh lemon juice	Samples in vinegar	Samples in club soda	Samples in distilled water
1					
2					
3					
4					
5					
6					
7					

0-7696-3429-X *Science Fair Projects: Volume 2*

Water Way To Treat Me

Step One }

MAKE AN OBSERVATION. Did you know that over 70% of our planet is covered with water, yet over one billion people living on our planet do not have a sustainable supply of safe drinking water? Most of the water on our planet is either too salty, frozen, or too deep in the earth's crust to make it suitable for human use. This leaves less than 1% of the earth's water to meet the needs of over six billion people. In addition, contaminants and pollutants caused by human activities are finding their way into our supply of usable water to further reduce the supply. Water is a nutrient that we cannot live without. It is a limited natural resource. Scientists are trying to find cost-effective ways to increase the amount of usable water available. One promising solution, although very costly, is desalination. Through desalination, water from the ocean is evaporated to separate it from salt and contaminants.

Step Two }

STATE THE PROBLEM AND POSE IT AS A RESEARCH QUESTION. Determine what effect desalination has on water's usability. In this investigation you will design and build a desalination plant and test fresh, untreated water and salt water to determine if using desalination can increase our water supply.

> What is the effect you observe?

> What is the possible cause of the effect?

> How can it be posed as a research question?

Step Three }

CONDUCT YOUR RESEARCH. Investigate the terms *potable water* and *desalination*. Also investigate different methods currently being used or proposed to desalinate unusable water. Write a summary of your findings to include in your presentation.

Step Four }

FORMULATE A HYPOTHESIS. Identify the independent variable you will change in your experiment. Identify the dependent variable that will be affected by what you change. Write a testable hypothesis that predicts the relationship between the independent and dependent variables. Your hypothesis should reflect a relationship between the type of water desalinated in your design and the effectiveness of the process in yielding usable water.

Step Five }

DESIGN AND CONDUCT YOUR EXPERIMENT.

A. Identify the variables you will keep the same during the experiment. Consider using the same desalination design, testing the same amount of unusable water, desalinating water under the same conditions (temperature, place, and amount of time water is allowed to evaporate), and using the same testing methods when the water has been processed.

B. Materials: materials to build your desalination plant; 2 empty 2-liter bottles; 2-liters of salt water; 2 liters of untreated lake, pond, or stream water; distilled water; sea salt; methylene blue (the high school chemistry teacher may have this); aquarium test strips for pH, nitrates, nitrites, ammonia, and hardness (available at most pet stores or on the Internet); small, clean glass baby food jars with no soap residue; and a thermometer

CAUTION: Do not drink any of the water used in this experiment.

C. Procedure

1. Write down all of the steps you use to build your water treatment system.

2. Prepare your salt water as follows:

    a. Fill an empty 2-liter bottle with warm tap water.

    b. Add 6 tablespoons of sea salt.

    c. Place the cap on the bottle and swirl the contents until most of the salt dissolves.

    d. Set the bottle aside and allow time for the rest of the salt to dissolve.

    e. Label the bottle Salt Water.

3. Find a source of untreated water, such as a pond or lake. Fill a 2-liter bottle with water from the untreated source and label it Untreated Water.

4. Fill one of the baby food jars with distilled water. Add 20 drops of methylene blue. This is the control. Cover the jar and observe the color. Record your observations in table 3.3 (p. 56).

5. Fill a second baby food jar with distilled water. Use an aquarium test strip according to the directions on the package. Record the results in the data table 3.4 (p. 56).

6. Use your desalination plant to process your untreated water. Put cleaned samples in two baby food jars.

7. Add 20 drops of methylene blue to one sample. Use an aquarium test strip to test the other sample. Record your data in the data tables.

8. Repeat steps 6–7 using the salt water.

9. Observe all the methylene blue jars every 10 minutes.

Note to experimenter: Methylene blue can be used to test water for bacteria. Bacteria cause methylene blue to change from blue to a colorless liquid as the oxygen in the water is depleted. The more bacteria a water sample contains, the faster the oxygen is depleted and the faster the color of the methylene blue breaks down.

D. Collect Data. Use the tables on page 56 to record your observations for one hour.

  0-7696-3429-X *Science Fair Projects: Volume 2*

Table 3.3　Testing with methylene blue

Type of water tested	Beginning color	Color after 10 minutes	Color after 20 minutes	Color after 30 minutes	Color after 40 minutes	Color after 50 minutes	Color after 60 minutes
Desalinated fresh water							
Desalinated salt water							
Distilled water							

Table 3.4　Testing with aquarium dip strips

Type of water tested	pH	Ammonia	Nitrate	Nitrite	Hardness
Desalinated fresh water					
Desalinated salt water					
Distilled water					

Step Six } **COMMUNICATE YOUR DATA IN AN APPROPRIATE MANNER.** To present your data, use a table (p. 57) that identifies the type of test used, communicates the result of the test on each sample, and describes the purpose of the test. Title your table.

Step Seven } **ANALYZE YOUR DATA TO DRAW CONCLUSIONS.** Based on your data, write a conclusion that summarizes your findings, states whether or not your hypothesis was correct, and identifies how your desalinated water samples compare to the distilled water when tested.

Step Eight } **EXPLAIN YOUR FINDINGS WITH AN INFERENCE.** Logically explain why the results of your experiment came out the way that they did, based on your research.

Alternatives and extensions

1. Design and build another plant to desalinate water using a different method. Compare the results using salt water or untreated water to determine if the method of desalination has an effect on whether the water is usable.

2. Research other water treatment systems and choose two to build and test using water from the same pond or lake. Then use the same tests to determine what effect the way the water is treated has on its safety for human use.

Type of test used	Untreated fresh water	Salt water	Description of test purpose and desired levels
Methylene blue			
pH			
Hardness			
Ammonia			
Nitrates			
Nitrites			

Water I Need To Grow?

Step One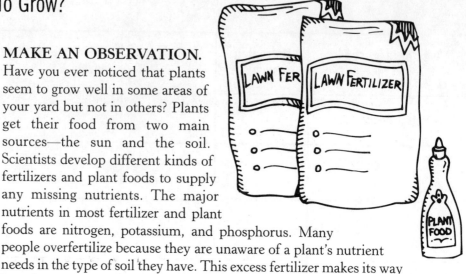

MAKE AN OBSERVATION.
Have you ever noticed that plants seem to grow well in some areas of your yard but not in others? Plants get their food from two main sources—the sun and the soil. Scientists develop different kinds of fertilizers and plant foods to supply any missing nutrients. The major nutrients in most fertilizer and plant foods are nitrogen, potassium, and phosphorus. Many people overfertilize because they are unaware of a plant's nutrient needs in the type of soil they have. This excess fertilizer makes its way into the water supply, creating a new problem—contaminated water.

Step Two

STATE THE PROBLEM AND POSE IT AS A RESEARCH QUESTION. Determine how much fertilizer is needed to accelerate seed germination. In this investigation, you will prepare solutions of plant food containing nitrogen, phosphorous, and potassium in varying concentrations to determine what effect each concentration has on the time a seed takes to germinate.

> What is the effect you observe?

> What is the possible cause of the effect?

> How can it be posed as a research question?

Step Three

CONDUCT YOUR RESEARCH. Investigate the terms *nitrates* and *phosphates*. Relate what effect these products have on plant growth and on water supplies. Also investigate the term *germination* and identify what seeds need to germinate. Write a summary of your findings to include in your presentation.

Step Four

FORMULATE A HYPOTHESIS. Identify the independent variable you will change in your experiment. Identify the dependent variable that will be affected by what you change. Write a testable hypothesis that predicts the relationship between the independent and dependent variables. Your hypothesis should predict which concentration of fertilizer causes your seeds to germinate the fastest.

Step Five } **DESIGN AND CONDUCT YOUR EXPERIMENT.**

A. Identify the variables you will keep the same during the experiment. Consider using the same type of seeds, allowing the seeds to germinate in the same place, adding the same amount of fertilizer solution to the germinating seeds, and using the same kind of fertilizer to make the solutions.

B. Materials: distilled water, fertilizer, a 100-ml graduated cylinder, 7 clean plastic bottles with tops, bean seeds, 7 petri dishes with lids, filter paper, scissors, 7 droppers, and a warm sunny place or a plant light

C. Procedure

1. Prepare the fertilizer solutions using this procedure.

    a. Add the amount of fertilizer shown in table 3.5 to the graduated cylinder.

    b. Add the amount of distilled water shown in the table.

    c. Pour the solution from the graduated cylinder into one of the plastic bottles.

    d. Put the cap on the bottle and shake the contents until all the fertilizer dissolves.

    e. Label the bottle with the concentration of the solution.

    f. Rinse out the graduated cylinder before preparing another solution.

    g. Fill the last bottle with distilled water only.

Table 3.5   Mixing ratios

Solution concentration	Fertilizer amount (ml)	Distilled water amount (ml)
5%	5	95
10%	10	90
15%	15	85
20%	20	80
25%	25	75
30%	30	70

2. Label 1 petri dish Distilled Water. Label the other petri dishes for the solution concentrations from the table above (5%, 10%, etc.).

3. Cut 2 pieces of filter paper to fit in each dish. Place 7 seeds in a vertical row on one filter paper in each dish. Then place 6 more seeds horizontally to create a + shape, as shown at right.

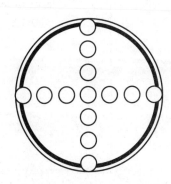

4. Moisten the seeds in the first dish with distilled water only. This is the control. Cover the moistened seeds with the second piece of filter paper and moisten again with distilled water.

5. Moisten the seeds in the second petri dish with 5% fertilizer solution. Cover the moistened seeds with the second piece of filter paper and moisten again with the 5% fertilizer solution.

6. Repeat steps 4–5 for the remaining fertilizer concentrations. Be sure to use the solution that matches the label on the petri dish.

7. Cover all 7 petri dishes and place them in a sunny place and leave them undisturbed for 5 days.

D. Collect Data. After the 5 days, check the seeds daily through day 12. Count the number of germinated seeds in each dish each day and moisten the seeds with the appropriate solution. Record your observations in data table 3.6 below.

Table 3.6   Seed germinating times

Day	Distilled water	5% solution	10% solution	15% solution	20% solution	25% solution	30% solution
6							
7							
8							
9							
10							
11							
12							

0-7696-3429-X *Science Fair Projects: Volume 2*

Step Six } **COMMUNICATE YOUR DATA IN AN APPROPRIATE MANNER.** Because the data collected in this investigation takes place over time, a multiple line graph is the best way to report your data. Label the *x*-axis "Day seeds were observed." Label the *y*-axis "Number of seeds germinated" and number from 0–13. Next, plot all the points from the data for the distilled water. When all of the points have been plotted, connect them in a line. Use a second color to plot the points for the data for the 5% solution and connect those points in a line. Use a different color for each data set. You should end up with seven lines in seven different colors. Provide a key and give your graph a title. If you wish, include the table of EPA standards for drinking water (p. 128) in your presentation.

Step Seven } **ANALYZE YOUR DATA TO DRAW CONCLUSIONS.** Based on your data, write a conclusion that summarizes your findings, states whether or not your hypothesis was correct, and identifies which fertilizer concentration germinated the most seeds in the least time. Also tell which fertilizer concentration germinated the fewest seeds.

Step Eight } **EXPLAIN YOUR FINDINGS WITH AN INFERENCE.** Logically explain why the results of your experiment came out the way that they did, based on your research.

Alternatives and extensions

1. Use a different type of fertilizer. Prepare the same concentrations (see Mixing ratios, p. 59) and use the same procedure to determine what effect the type of fertilizer used has on the amount of time it takes to germinate bean seeds.

2. Use a different type of fertilizer and concentrations but then use different seeds to determine what effect the type of seed has on the time it takes a seed to germinate.

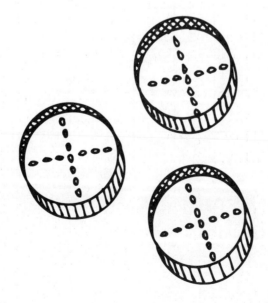

0-7696-3429-X *Science Fair Projects: Volume 2*

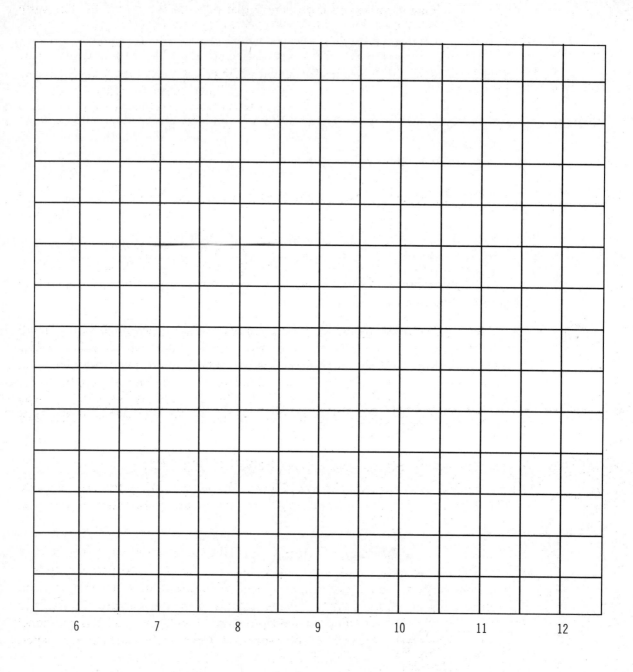

The Paper Caper

Step One } **MAKE AN OBSERVATION.** On a trip to a local landfill, you can see that most of the waste is made up of paper. According to the EPA (the Environmental Protection Agency), 38% of the total weight of all the waste in a landfill consists of paper. This may surprise you if you know that paper is also one of the top waste products recycled. Over 40% of the paper we use gets recycled, yet paper still fills our landfills.

Step Two } **STATE THE PROBLEM AND POSE IT AS A RESEARCH QUESTION.** Find out why so much paper still ends up in landfills. Conduct an investigation to determine the effect of the type of paper on its recyclability. In this investigation you will explore whether different types of paper can be made into new, usable paper.

> What is the effect you observe?

> What is the possible cause of the effect?

> How can it be posed as a research question?

Step Three } **CONDUCT YOUR RESEARCH.** Investigate how paper is made, how paper is recycled, how paper is treated to make it shiny, glossy, colored, white, etc., and what recycled paper products are available. Write a summary of your findings to include in your presentation.

Step Four } **FORMULATE A HYPOTHESIS.** Identify the independent variable you will change in your experiment. Identify the dependent variable that will be affected by what you change. Write a testable hypothesis that predicts the relationship between the independent and dependent variable. Your hypothesis can be a positive statement that predicts a relationship between the type of paper and its recyclability into new paper or a negative statement that predicts no connection between these two variables.

Step Five } **DESIGN AND CONDUCT YOUR EXPERIMENT.**

A. Identify the variables you will keep the same during the experiment. Consider using the same process to make new paper and the same test to determine the paper's usability.

B. Materials: 5 different types of paper (glossy magazine paper, newspaper, colored construction paper, notebook or printer paper, old cards, recycled paper, tissue paper, paper towels, toilet paper, etc.), a clean sponge, fiberglass window screening, a wood picture frame, a plastic basin/tub large enough to totally immerse the frame, a blender or food processor, 1 yard of white felt or flannel fabric, 2 cookie sheets, staples or tacks, stacks of newspaper, and liquid starch

C. Procedure

1. Stretch the fiberglass screen tightly over the frame and staple the edges of the screen to secure it to the frame. Make the screen as tight as possible. This is your mold.

2. Cut 2 fabric squares (felt or flannel) a little larger than the mold.

3. Place 1 fabric square on the back (bottom) of a cookie sheet and set it aside.

4. Choose one type of paper and tear it into small pieces no larger than a postage stamp, until you have about 1 cup of torn paper.

5. Place the torn paper in the blender and add four cups of warm water.

6. Start the blender on low. Increase the speed until the paper becomes pulpy, looks well blended, and no flakes of paper are visible.

7. Pour the blended paper into the basin and stir it with a clean spoon to evenly distribute the fibers.

8. Add 2 tablespoons of liquid starch to the paper pulp. Stir until evenly mixed.

9. Slide the mold into the pulp (staple-side up) and level it while it is submerged. Gently wiggle it side to side until the pulp layer on top of the screen looks even.

10. Slowly lift the mold (keeping it horizontal) out of the water. Allow it to drain until the water stops dripping.

11. Gently lift the mold out of the basin and place one edge on the edge of the fabric square on the cookie sheet. Gently turn the mold over, making sure the paper is directly against the fabric.

12. Use a sponge to press out as much more water as possible. Wring the excess water back into the basin.

13. Holding the fabric square flat, slowly lift the edge of the mold, transferring the new paper to the fabric. (If the paper sticks to the mold, you may have pulled too fast or may not have pressed out enough water.)

14. Use the sponge to gently press out any bubbles and loose edges of the paper.

15. Cover your new paper with the other square of fabric. Use the other cookie sheet to press more water out of the stack. You may wish to do this outside or in the bathtub.

16. Transfer the sandwiched paper and fabric to a stack of newspaper and allow it to dry. This may take a day or two.

17. Peel the dry new paper from the fabric. Use an ink pen to label the paper telling what type of paper you used to make it.

18. Clean all the tools and repeat steps 3–17 for the remaining types of paper.

19. Set all of the recycled papers side by side and use the quality scale in table 3.7 (p. 65) to rate each paper's usability.

D. Collect Data.

Rate the quality of the paper from 1–5, with 1 the lowest score and 5 the highest score.

Table 3.7 Rating recycled paper usability

Type of paper used in recycling process					
Smoothness: Run your hand over its surface.					
Evenness: Hold the paper up to the light and notice how the light shines through.					
Strength: Mark the paper with a pencil and then erase the mark.					
Flexibility: Fold the paper in half and in half again. Consider how easy it is to fold and how well the folds hold.					
Density: Cut a 1" x 4" strip of paper. Wet it and place it on a cookie sheet in a 400° oven for 15 minutes. The least dense paper will curl the most.					
Capillary action: Write on the paper with a felt-tip marker to determine if and how much the ink bleeds.					
Total score: Add the points scored to find the paper's usability score.					

Step Six } **COMMUNICATE YOUR DATA IN AN APPROPRIATE MANNER.**
Use a bar graph (p. 67) to compare the total scores for each type of paper. Label the *x*-axis "Type of paper recycled" and write the types of the papers used under the bars. Label the *y*-axis "Paper's usability score." Number this axis by ones. Color a bar to communicate each paper's total score. Add a key and a title to your graph.

0-7696-3429-X *Science Fair Projects: Volume 2*

Step Seven } **ANALYZE YOUR DATA TO DRAW CONCLUSIONS.** Based on your data, write a conclusion that summarizes your findings, states whether or not your hypothesis was correct, and identifies which paper produced the most usable recycled paper. Also tell which paper produced the least usable recycled paper.

Step Eight } **EXPLAIN YOUR FINDINGS WITH AN INFERENCE.** Logically explain why the results of your experiment came out the way that they did, based on your research. Include reasons some types of paper are not recycled and why you think so much paper ends up in landfills.

Alternatives and extensions

1. Paper is generally made from trees, but it can also be made from other materials, such as dryer lint, absorbent cotton, and old rags. Use the same procedure to make paper from alternative materials to determine how the type of material used affects the usability of the paper made.

2. Combine different types of paper in the paper-making process to determine the best ratios for producing quality papers. Rate them with the usability chart (p.65).

0-7696-3429-X *Science Fair Projects: Volume 2*

Paper or Plastic Bags

Step One } **MAKE AN OBSERVATION.** The grocery bagger asks, "Paper or plastic?" Do you ever wonder what difference it makes? The Sierra Club, an environmental organization, says it makes a lot of difference. Plastic bags are a petroleum product. Four out of five people use plastic instead of paper. Plastic bags are lighter, have handles that make them easier to carry, and are thought to be more hygienic. Like paper bags, plastic bags can be recycled. Recycling one ton of plastic bags saves eleven barrels of oil. Since Americans use fourteen million plastic shopping bags each year, recycling them could save a lot of oil. But do most people throw their plastic bags away instead of recycling them? When plastic bags end up in a landfill, it takes ten to twenty years for them to decompose. And light plastic bags are carried by the wind into the natural environment where they harm wildlife.

Step Two } **STATE THE PROBLEM AND POSE IT AS A RESEARCH QUESTION.** Find out if and why most people seem to prefer plastic grocery bags over paper bags. In this investigation, you will survey people to determine which type of bag they prefer, why they have this preference, and what they do with the bags when they get them home.

> What is the effect you observe?

> What is the possible cause of the effect?

> How can it be posed as a research question?

Step Three } **CONDUCT YOUR RESEARCH.** Investigate how plastic and paper grocery bags are made, how each is recycled, what effect each has on the environment, and what recycling incentives and programs are available in your area. Also investigate the cost of each as a possible reason stores want to use plastic more than paper. Write a summary of your findings to include in your presentation.

Step Four } **FORMULATE A HYPOTHESIS.** Identify the independent variable you will change in your experiment. Identify the dependent variable that will be affected by what you change. Write a testable hypothesis that predicts the relationship between the independent and dependent variables. Your hypothesis can be a positive statement predicting that most people prefer plastic grocery bags over paper bags and why you think this is. Or make a neutral statement predicting that people do not have a preference and state why you think this is. You can also choose to make a negative prediction that people prefer paper bags but stores promote using plastic ones.

Step Five } **DESIGN AND CONDUCT YOUR EXPERIMENT.**

A. Identify the variables you will keep the same during the experiment. Consider surveying people in the same area using the same questions.

B. Materials: 200 survey participants, data table 3.8 (p. 69)

C. Procedure

1. Contact grocery stores to find 2 that offer both paper and plastic bags. Get permission from the managers to conduct your investigation.

2. Go to the selected stores. Use table 3.8 below or create your own. Survey 200 people. Record their responses using tally marks. You may need to return to the stores several times to collect all of your data. Use a new copy of the table for each store and for each time you go. Total your responses frequently so you know when you reach 200.

D. Collect data.

Table 3.8   Paper or plastic?

Store _____ Date/time _____

Question	Response	Response	Response	Response	Response
What type of bag do you prefer?	Paper	Plastic	Other		
Number of people w/ response					
Why do you choose that?	Easier to carry	Better for the environment	Doesn't leak	More convenient	Other
Number of people w/ response					
What will you do with the bag after using?	Throw it away	Recycle or reuse it	Other		
Number of people w/ response					

0-7696-3429-X *Science Fair Projects: Volume 2*

Step Six } **COMMUNICATE YOUR DATA IN AN APPROPRIATE MANNER.**
This data is best communicated using percents. Use three circle graphs (p. 72) to report your findings. To calculate the part of a circle for each response, use the formula below. Complete table 3.9 to make the calculations. Make a separate circle graph for each question. Label each section and add a title to each graph.

$$(n \times 360°) \div y = d,$$

in which n = number of tallies per response, y = total number surveyed and d = degrees of circle needed. Round your answer to the nearest whole number.

Table 3.9   Calculations

Question					
What type of bag?	Paper	Plastic	Other		
n					
x 360°					
÷ y					
= d					
Why bag was chosen?	Easier to carry	Better for the environment	Doesn't leak	More convenient	Other
n					
x 360°					
÷ y					
= d					
What they will do with the bag when emptied?	Throw it away	Recycle or reuse it	Other		
n					
x 360°					
÷ y					
= d					

Published by Milestone. Copyright protected.

0-7696-3429-X *Science Fair Projects: Volume 2*

Step Seven } **ANALYZE YOUR DATA TO DRAW CONCLUSIONS.** Based on your data, write a conclusion that states whether or not your hypothesis was correct, identifies which type of bag people preferred most, why they preferred it, and what they will do with the bag when it is empty.

Step Eight } **EXPLAIN YOUR FINDINGS WITH AN INFERENCE.** Logically explain why the results of your experiment came out the way they did, based on your research. Infer whether you think these responses are related to the recycling programs available in your area and/or to the costs of paper and plastic bags to the stores.

Alternatives and extensions

1. Choose another type of packaging, such as plastic bottles and aluminum cans used for sodas, and conduct the same type of survey to determine what effect the type of packaging has on the customers' buying preferences.

2. Conduct a regional study by surveying members of your family or acquaintances who live in different areas of the U.S. Call them and ask the same questions in this survey to determine what effect geography has on the type of grocery bag they prefer to use. Also ask what type of incentives and recycling programs are available in their areas.

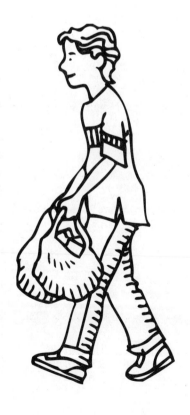

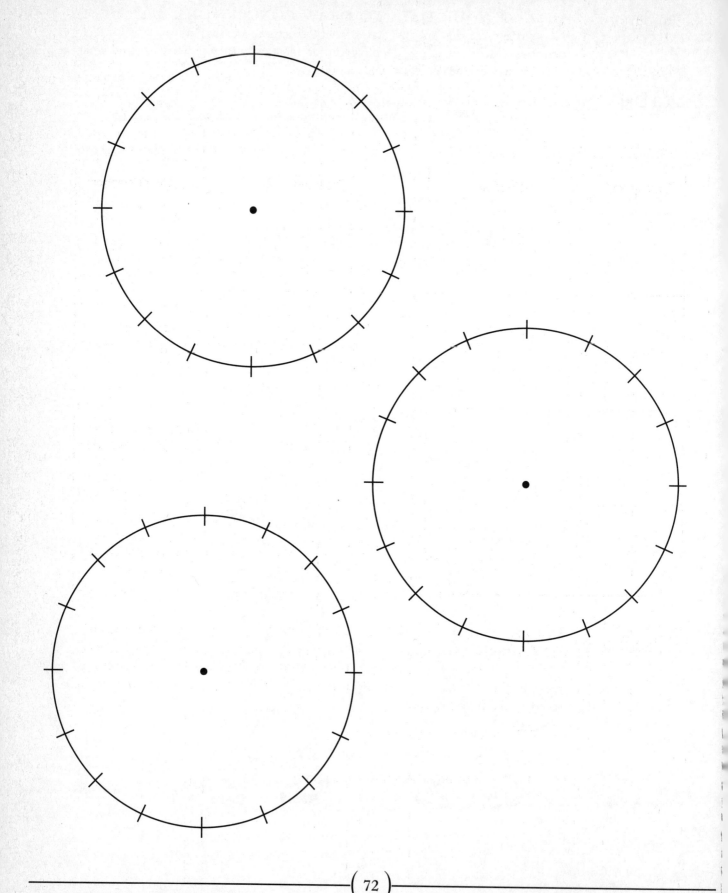

A Clean Solution

Step One } **MAKE AN OBSERVATION.** Do you know why we use different cleaners for different cleaning tasks? Different types of soil respond to cleaners that are either basic or acidic. Look at table 4.1 below.

Table 4.1   Unwanted soil types

Type of soil	Definition	Examples	Best type of cleaner
Inorganic	Matter that was never living and contains no carbon	Scale and lime deposits, water spots, rust, corrosion, minerals, rock formations, and dirt	Acidic cleaners with pH levels from 1–6.9
Organic	Matter that was once living and contains carbon	Body oils, animal fats such as kitchen grease, carbohydrates and proteins such as those found in food, mold, yeast, mildew, odor-causing bacteria, animal waste, germs, and soap scum	Alkaline (basic) cleaners with pH levels from 7.1–14
Combination	Organic and inorganic matter	Combinations of materials above	Alkalines and solvents for mostly inorganic soils, and acids and solvents for mostly organic soils
Petroleum	Petroleum products or distillates	Motor oil, axle and automotive grease, waxes, gums, cosmetics, and scuff marks	A petroleum-based solvent (no pH level because the soils do not contain water molecules)

Step Two } **STATE THE PROBLEM AND POSE IT AS A RESEARCH QUESTION.** Determine how the pH of a household cleaner determines its effectiveness in cleaning different soils. In this investigation, use an indicator to measure the pH level of different cleaners to determine if they can clean the type of soil they claim they to clean.

> What is the effect you observe?

> What is the possible cause of the effect?

> How can it be posed as a research question?

Step Three } **CONDUCT YOUR RESEARCH.** Investigate the terms *pH, indicators, acids, bases, alkaline solutions, solvents,* and *soils*. Also investigate cleaning research. Write a summary of what you find out. You may wish to include table 4.1, Unwanted soil types (p. 73), in your presentation.

Step Four } **FORMULATE A HYPOTHESIS.** Identify the independent variable that you will change in your experiment. Identify the dependent variable that will be affected by what you change. Write a testable hypothesis that predicts the relationship between the independent and dependent variables. Your hypothesis may be a positive statement predicting a connection between the types of soils cleaners advertise to clean and pH levels of the cleaners, or a negative statement predicting no connection between the two variables.

Step Five } **DESIGN AND CONDUCT YOUR EXPERIMENT.**

A. Identify the variables you will keep the same during the experiment. Consider using the same type of indicator to test pH levels, using containers made of the same material to test cleaners, testing each cleaner in its own container, testing the same amounts of cleaner, and testing all of the cleaners at full strength.

B. Materials: red cabbage juice indicator strips or other pH indicator, various household cleaners (toilet bowl cleaner, soap scum cleaner, degreaser, disinfectant, mouthwash, etc.), pipettes or eye droppers, and safety goggles

C. Procedure

1. Follow this procedure to make your red-cabbage indicator strips.

    a. Cut 1/2 a head of red cabbage into small pieces.

    b. Place the cut cabbage in a blender and completely cover with hot water.

    c. Blend on high for 3–5 minutes until the water turns purple and the cabbage turns to pulp.

    d. Strain the mixture through a colander lined with a coffee filter.

    e. Strain the mixture a second time to ensure that all of the cabbage pulp is removed.

    f. Dip several clean coffee filters in the strained cabbage juice and set them on a piece of wax paper to dry.

    g. When the filters are dry, cut them in strips.

2. Identify the name of the cleaner you are testing. Read the label to determine what type of unwanted soil it claims to clean. Record both pieces of information in data table 4.3 on page 76.

CAUTION: Wear safety goggles and protective gloves when working with these chemicals.

3. Wearing safety goggles and gloves, carefully use a pipette to collect some of the cleaner. Drop it on one of the cabbage-juice indicator strips.

4. Use the indicator scale below to determine the pH based on the color the strip turns. Record this information in table 4.3.

5. Dispose of the testing strip. Repeat steps 3 and 4 two more times on the same cleaner.

6. Based on the results of all three trials, determine if the cleaner is an acid, a base, or a solvent. A solvent will show a neutral pH of 7 and will feel oily.

7. Decide whether the cleaner is capable of cleaning the type of soil claimed for it, based on your findings. Write your evaluation in table 4.3.

8. Repeat steps 2–7 for the remaining cleaners.

D. Collect data.

Table 4.2   Red cabbage pH scale

Type of solution	pH	Indicator color
Strong acid	1	Orange
	2	Orange-red
	3	Red
	4	Bright pink
	5	Magenta
Weak acid	6	Purplish-pink
Neutral	7	Purple
Weak base	8	Blue
	9	Turquoise
	10	Blue-green
	11	Green-blue
	12	Green
	13	Yellow-green
Strong base	14	Yellow

Published by Milestone. Copyright protected.

0-7696-3429-X *Science Fair Projects: Volume 2*

Table 4.3 Cleaner Observations

Name of cleaner	Type of soil it claims to clean	pH trial 1	pH trial 2	pH trial 3	Acid, base, or solvent?	Evaluation

Step Six } **COMMUNICATE YOUR DATA IN AN APPROPRIATE MANNER.** Because the observations made in this experiment depended on the cleaners used, your observation table should be included in your presentation. Also display the red cabbage indicator chart (table 4.2) used for your measurements.

Step Seven } **ANALYZE YOUR DATA TO DRAW CONCLUSIONS.** Based on your data, write a conclusion that summarizes your findings, states whether or not your hypothesis was correct, and identifies how average consumers could find out if a cleaner stands up to its claims.

Step Eight } **EXPLAIN YOUR FINDINGS WITH AN INFERENCE.** Logically explain why the results of your experiment came out the way they did, based on your research.

Alternatives and extensions

1. Compare similar cleaners made by different companies. Determine whether the same product made by a different company is more or less effective at cleaning what it claims to clean.

2. Look for more environmentally friendly cleaners, such as vinegar, and compare their cleaning abilities to the cleaning products available at your local retailer.

An Itchy Problem

Step One }

MAKE AN OBSERVATION. Dandruff is an itchy problem. Also known as *seborrheic dermatitis*, some scientists hypothesize that it is caused by an overgrowth of yeast normally found on our scalps. As yeast may only be one cause of dandruff, scientists have worked to develop many different brands of dandruff shampoos containing different active ingredients to combat the problems caused by an itchy, flakey scalp.

Step Two }

STATE THE PROBLEM AND POSE IT AS A RESEARCH QUESTION. How is the consumer to choose from all the different types of dandruff shampoos? In this investigation, you will experiment with different brands of dandruff shampoos containing different ingredients to find out which ingredient slows or prevents yeast growth.

> What is the effect you observe?

> What is the possible cause of the effect?

> How can it be posed as a research question?

Step Three }

CONDUCT YOUR RESEARCH. Investigate the terms *dandruff* and *seborrheic dermatitis* to find out what may cause it and to learn ways it can be prevented or eliminated. Write a summary of your findings to include in your presentation.

Step Four }

FORMULATE A HYPOTHESIS. Identify the independent variable you will change in your experiment. Identify the dependent variable that will be affected by what you change. Write a testable hypothesis that predicts the relationship between the independent and dependent variables. Your hypothesis may be a positive statement predicting that a specific ingredient works better than others at inhibiting yeast growth, a general statement predicting that all ingredients work about the same to inhibit yeast growth, or a negative statement predicting that dandruff shampoos purchased at the store do not inhibit yeast growth.

Step Five }

DESIGN AND CONDUCT YOUR EXPERIMENT.

A. Identify the variables you will keep the same during the experiment. Consider using the same amount of shampoo and water in each container, using containers made of the same material, placing containers in the same place at the same temperature, and using the same type and size of balloons to measure yeast growth.

B. Materials: 5 varieties of dandruff shampoo containing different ingredients; active dry yeast; 11 clean, glass soda bottles; sugar; a tablespoon; a teaspoon; a gallon of distilled water; a funnel; 11 large latex balloons; a metric measuring tape; and a warm, dark place where the bottles will not be disturbed

C. Procedure

1. Inflate the balloons to stretch them, then let the air out and set them aside.

2. Fill the first bottle half full of distilled water at room temperature. Use the funnel to add one tablespoon of sugar to the bottle.

3. Place your hand firmly over the top of the bottle and shake to dissolve the sugar.

4. Use the funnel to add 1 teaspoon of active dry yeast to the sugar water. Quickly secure a latex balloon over the top of the bottle. This bottle is your control. Label it distilled water.

5. For each shampoo, fill 2 soda bottles half full with distilled water at room temperature. Then use the funnel to add 1 tablespoon of sugar to each bottle.

6. Label the bottles with the names of the dandruff shampoos. To each bottle, add 2 teaspoons of a shampoo. Place your hand firmly over the top and mix the ingredients. Secure a balloon over each bottle.

7. Carefully move all the bottles to a warm, dark place where they will not be disturbed for the next 5 hours.

8. Check the bottles after 30 minutes and then every hour to determine when the balloons pop upright. Record this information in table 4.4 on page 80.

9. Continue monitoring the bottles every hour. Use the measuring tape to measure the circumference of each balloon. Record the measurements in your data table.

10. At the end of 5 hours, measure and record the circumference of each balloon. Take apart the bottles and balloons. Clean the bottles and throw way the balloons.

11. In table 4.5 (p. 80), calculate the average circumference of the balloons for each brand of shampoo after 5 hours. To calculate the average, add the final measurements for the 2 bottles of each shampoo and divide by 2.

Note to experimenter: Yeast produces both carbon dioxide and alcohol as it grows. The CO_2 gas causes the balloon to expand as the yeast grows. When you remove the balloon, you may notice that the solution smells like alcohol. The process by which yeast produces both CO_2 and alcohol is commonly called *fermentation*. In bottles where the yeast was not as active the balloon will not expand as much and the alcohol smell will not be as strong.

D. Collect data. Use the data tables on page 80.

Table 4.4   Balloon expansion rates

Note when the balloon first moves to an upright position. Then measure the circumference in subsequent observations.

Shampoo brand	30 minutes	1 hour	2 hours	3 hours	4 hours	5 hours

Table 4.5   Average balloon expansion

Shampoo brand	Final circumference bottle 1 (cm)	Final circumference bottle 2 (cm)	Total of circumferences	÷ 2	Average circumference (cm)

Step Six } **COMMUNICATE YOUR DATA IN AN APPROPRIATE MANNER.** Because you are comparing measurements of gas produced as the yeast grew, you may use a bar graph to report your findings (see p. 82). The x-axis should be labeled "Name of shampoo tested." Distilled water and the names of the shampoos should be written along this axis. Label the y-axis "Balloon's average circumference after 5 hours (cm)." Number this using the smallest increments possible. For each shampoo tested, make a bar that communicates the average balloon circumference. Add a title that communicates what your graph is about.

Step Seven } **ANALYZE YOUR DATA TO DRAW CONCLUSIONS.** Based on your data, write a conclusion that summarizes your findings, states whether or not your hypothesis was correct, and identifies which shampoo worked best as shown by the smallest amount of gas produced. Identify which active ingredients this shampoo contains. Then identify the least effective shampoo as shown by the greatest amount of gas production. Identify its active ingredients.

Step Eight } **EXPLAIN YOUR FINDINGS WITH AN INFERENCE.** Logically explain why the results of your experiment came out the way they did, based on your research.

Alternative and extension

Conduct the same experiment using one brand of dandruff shampoo and other types of shampoo, such as shampoos formulated for dry hair, baby shampoo, or conditioning shampoos, to determine if the ingredients in dandruff shampoos are more effective than ingredients in other shampoos at preventing or slowing the growth of yeast.

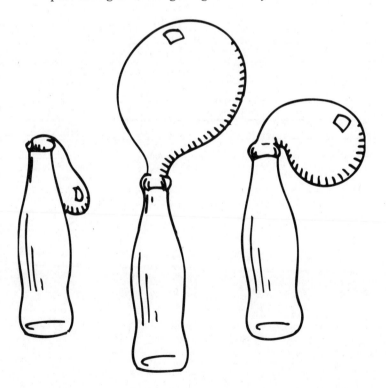

Distilled water

0-7696-3429-X *Science Fair Projects: Volume 2*

How Do You Spell Relief?

Step One } **MAKE AN OBSERVATION.** Lots of different products claim to relieve heartburn. Over-the-counter antacids work by using a basic active ingredient to neutralize stomach acid. But how do we know which antacid will work the best?

Step Two } **STATE THE PROBLEM AND POSE IT AS A RESEARCH QUESTION.** Different antacids contain different active ingredients or combinations of ingredients to neutralize stomach acid. In this investigation, you will test antacids with different active ingredients to determine their effectiveness in neutralizing stomach acid.

> What is the effect you observe?

> What is the possible cause of the effect?

> How can it be posed as a research question?

Step Three } **CONDUCT YOUR RESEARCH.** Investigate the terms *antacid*, *pH*, *acid*, *base*, *neutralization*, *heartburn*, and *stomach acid*. Investigate how antacids work and what causes excess stomach acid that leads to heartburn. Write a summary of your findings to include in your presentation.

Step Four } **FORMULATE A HYPOTHESIS.** Identify the independent variable you will change in your experiment. Identify the dependent variable that will be affected by what you change. Write a testable hypothesis that predicts the relationship between the independent and dependent variables. Your hypothesis may either be a positive statement that predicts that a specific ingredient will work better than others at neutralizing stomach acid, a general statement that predicts that all ingredients will work about the same to neutralize stomach acid, or a negative statement that predicts that over-the-counter antacids are not effective at neutralizing stomach acid.

Step Five } **DESIGN AND CONDUCT YOUR EXPERIMENT.**

A. Identify the variables you will keep the same during the experiment. Consider using one dose of each antacid tested, adding the antacid to the stomach solution in the same manner, using the same amount of stomach acid, and using the same size and type of containers throughout the experiment.

B. Materials: 5 over-the-counter antacids containing different active ingredients; a mortar and pestle or plastic freezer bags and a large metal spoon; red cabbage juice indicator; 2 clean 12-oz. clear glass bottles; 10 large round latex balloons; a metric measuring tape; a stopwatch or timer; 1 liter of 5% vinegar solution; a graduated cylinder; a dropper or pipette; and 2 funnels

C. Procedure

1. Inflate the balloons to stretch them out, let the air out, and set them aside.

2. Prepare your red cabbage juice as directed below:

    a. Cut half a head of red cabbage into small pieces.

    b. Place the cut cabbage in a blender and completely cover with hot water.

    c. Blend on high for 3–5 minutes until the water turns purple and the cabbage turns to pulp.

    d. Strain the mixture through a colander lined with a coffee filter.

    e. Strain the mixture a second time to ensure that all the cabbage pulp is removed. Store the mixture in a clean bottle with a lid.

3. Write the name and active ingredient(s) of the antacid being tested in data tables 4.6 and 4.7 (p. 85).

4. Use the mortar and pestle to crush one dose (according to the package) of the first antacid. Or place the dose in a freezer bag and use the back of a metal spoon to crush the tablet(s).

5. Use one funnel to place the crushed antacid in a balloon. Set the balloon aside.

6. Use the graduated cylinder to measure 100 ml of 5% vinegar solution. The vinegar represents stomach acid.

7. Use the other funnel to pour the vinegar into a clean glass bottle. Use a dropper or pipette to add .5 ml of red cabbage juice to the vinegar. Note the pH of the solution (use the scale on p. 75) and record it in your table.

8. Carefully stretch the mouth of the balloon containing the first antacid over the neck of the bottle of vinegar "stomach acid." Make sure the antacid does not go into the bottle until you are ready to start timing.

9. Raise the balloon to empty the antacid into the vinegar and begin timing. Stop the timer when the solution in the bottle turns purple, indicating that it is neutral. Record the time in table 4.6.

10. Allow the bottle to sit for 10 minutes. Then use the measuring tape to measure the circumference of the balloon. This measurement indicates how much gas was produced as a result of the reaction. Record your measurement in table 4.7.

11. Repeat steps 4–10 using the second bottle and another dose of the same antacid.

12. Carefully remove and dispose of the balloons. Pour the vinegar solutions down the drain and flush with water.

13. Wash both bottles thoroughly with warm water and a bottle brush to remove any sediment or residue and let them dry completely.

14. Repeat steps 3–13 to test the other 4 antacids.

D. Collect data.

Average the data you collected for each antacid and record the calculations in the data tables below.

Table 4.6　Antacid neutralizing times

Name of antacid	Active ingredient(s)	Time to neutralize trial 1	Time to neutralize trial 2	Total time trials 1 and 2	÷ 2	Average time to neutralize	Average time in seconds
					÷ 2		
					÷ 2		
					÷ 2		
					÷ 2		
					÷ 2		

Table 4.7　Amount of gas produced

Name of antacid	Active ingredient(s)	Balloons circumference trial 1	Balloons circumference trial 2	Total circumference trials 1 and 2	÷ 2	Average circumference
					÷ 2	
					÷ 2	
					÷ 2	
					÷ 2	
					÷ 2	

0-7696-3429-X *Science Fair Projects: Volume 2*

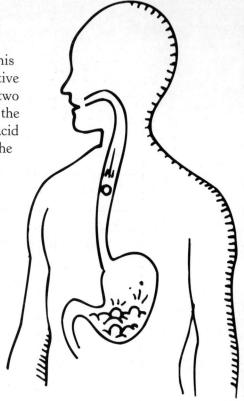

Step Six }

COMMUNICATE YOUR DATA IN AN APPROPRIATE MANNER. In this investigation you collected two sets of descriptive data, so two bar graphs are appropriate. Use two copies of the graph at the top of page 87. For the data in table 4.6, label the x-axis "Name of antacid tested." Write the names of the antacids along the axis. Label the y-axis "Time to neutralize (secs.)." Look at the range of average times from lowest to highest and decide how to number the y-axis. Add a title to the graph.

For the data in table 4.7, label the x-axis "Name of antacid." Label the y-axis "Balloon circumference (cm)." Look at the range of average balloon circumferences from lowest to highest to decide how to number the y-axis. Add a title to the graph. Include a table that identifies the name of the antacids tested and their active ingredients (see bottom of p. 87).

Step Seven }

ANALYZE YOUR DATA TO DRAW CONCLUSIONS. Based on your data, write a conclusion that summarizes your findings, states whether or not your hypothesis was correct, and identifies which antacid and active ingredient neutralized the acid in the shortest time and which took the longest. Identify which antacid produced the least amount of gas, as shown by the smallest balloon, and which produced the most gas, as shown by the largest balloon.

Step Eight }

EXPLAIN YOUR FINDINGS WITH AN INFERENCE. Logically explain why the results of your experiment came out the way they did, based on your research.

Alternative and extension

Find natural remedies, such as baking soda or peppermint tea, and conduct the same investigation to determine if natural remedies are as effective in neutralizing stomach acid as over-the-counter remedies.

0-7696-3429-X *Science Fair Projects: Volume 2*

Active ingredients of tested antacids

Name of antacid	Active ingredient/s

It's A Small World

Step One }

MAKE AN OBSERVATION. Have you noticed how many antibacterial products are available in stores? The widespread use of these products may not be best for general health. Most plants and animals depend on some kinds of bacteria to live. Bacteria aid the digestion of food, allowing organisms to absorb nutrients. In some cases, the bacteria are the food, as in yogurt. Not all bacteria are beneficial. Between 1% and 5% of bacteria cause harmful diseases in organisms and can even be fatal. Many creatures have adapted defenses against harmful bacteria. Humans, besides having natural defenses, also rely on good bacteria to prevent the growth of harmful bacteria. The beneficial bacteria occupy space and thus prevent harmful bacteria from colonizing, and they produce acids that kill harmful bacteria.

So why do we need antibacterial products? Antibacterial products were developed for hospital workers, to reduce the number of strep and staph infections caused by harmful bacteria. Triclosan, a pesticide effective against a few species of bacteria and fungi, is the active ingredient in these products. Scientists wonder what effect the overuse of triclosan will have on its usefulness against harmful bacteria.

Step Two }

STATE THE PROBLEM AND POSE IT AS A RESEARCH QUESTION. Evaluate the benefits and costs associated with antibacterial products. In this investigation, you will grow bacteria from your body on slices of potato. Then you will treat the slices with antibacterial products to determine what effect the products have on inhibiting bacterial growth.

> What is the effect you observe?

> What is the possible cause of the effect?

> How can it be posed as a research question?

Step Three }

CONDUCT YOUR RESEARCH. Investigate the terms *triclosan, pathogenic bacteria, strep, staph,* and *infectious diseases.* Investigate ways bacteria help us stay healthy and what effects killing them may have. Write a summary of your findings to include in your presentation.

Step Six } **FORMULATE A HYPOTHESIS.** Identify the independent variable you will change in your experiment. Identify the dependent variable that will be affected by what you change. Write a testable hypothesis that predicts the relationship between the independent and dependent variables. Your hypothesis may be a positive statement that predicts that all antibacterial products tested will inhibit the growth of all bacteria, a general statement that predicts that all the antibacterial products will inhibit the growth of some of the bacteria, or a negative statement that predicts that all of the bacterial products have lost their effectiveness to inhibit bacterial growth.

Step Five } **DESIGN AND CONDUCT YOUR EXPERIMENT.**

A. Identify the variables you will keep the same during the experiment. Consider using the same potato to make potato slices, treating the potato with the same amount of bacteria from the same place, using the same dishes to grow bacteria in, growing bacteria in the same location, using the same method to treat the potato slices, and using the same method to calculate the amount of bacteria growth.

B. Materials: 1 large potato; a sharp kitchen knife; 6 different antibacterial products (liquid hand soap, dishwashing soap, mouthwash, etc.); 7 clear plastic deli containers with lids (diameters of about 4 1/2"); distilled water; sterile swabs; a warm, dark place; 6 clean test tubes; 6 clean droppers; test tube stoppers; a fine-point permanent marker; a metric ruler; paper towels; sugar water; and a thick plastic trash bag

C. Procedure

1. Begin this experiment by going without bathing or using deodorant for 24 hours. This means no shower before you go to bed and no deodorant when you get up.

2. When you are ready to begin the experiment, peel the potato and cut it into seven 2-cm-thick slices. Try cutting from the middle of the potato to ensure that all of the slices are about the same size.

3. Cut several layers of paper towels to fit the bottom of each deli container. Cover the layers with a sugar-water solution. Lay 1 potato slice in each container on top of the soaked paper towels.

4. Use a sterile swab to collect bacteria from your armpit by rubbing the swab over your skin. Transfer the bacteria to one of the potato slices by rubbing the swab in a zigzag motion over the potato to cover as much area as possible. Quickly put the lid on the container.

5. Repeat step 4 for the other slices, using a new sterile swab each time. Label the containers A–G.

6. Put the treated potato slices in a warm dark place.

7. Allow the bacteria to grow on the potato slices for at least 24 hours.

8. Check your potato slices after 24 hours for bacterial growth (tiny, round circles that may be orange or shiny white). Without removing the lid, use a fine-point permanent marker to outline the bacterial colonies observed and use a metric ruler to measure their diameter in millimeters. Record the number of colonies and their color in table 4.8 (p. 91) and record the measured diameter of each colony.

Note to experimenter : If no or little bacterial growth is observed, return the samples and wait another 24 hours.

9. Prepare your antibacterial solutions by filling a test tube half full of distilled water and adding 4 drops of the antibacterial product. Put the stopper on the test tube and swish the contents to mix the solution.

10. Use a dropper. Take the lid off one potato container and quickly place 2 drops of the antibacterial solution on each bacteria colony. Replace the lid and label the container with the name of the antibacterial product you used.

11. Repeat steps 9–10 with the remaining 5 antibacterial products.

12. Treat the seventh container with a few drops of distilled water and label it Control Specimen.

CAUTION: Keep all the lids secured to avoid contamination.

13. Return the containers to the warm, dark place and observe them every morning and afternoon for the next 2 days. Without removing the lids, mark and measure the diameters of the bacteria colonies and record your observations in the table.

14. At the end of the 3 days, after you record all your data, place all of the sealed containers in a thick trash bag. Tie the bag and dispose of it in an outdoor trash can.

15. Transfer the data that shows the diameters of the bacterial colonies at the end of day 1 and the diameters at the end of day 3 to table 4.9 (p. 93). Find the difference between the two values and record it as either a positive number to indicate an increase in the bacteria or as a negative number to indicate a decrease in bacteria.

D. Collect data. Use data tables 4.8 and 4.9 on pages 91–93 to record what happens during your experiment.

Table 4.8   Watching bacteria grow

Day	Antibacterial product	Observations	Measurements (mm)
After 24 hours (Day 1)	A. Untreated		
	B. Untreated		
	C. Untreated		
	D. Untreated		
	E. Untreated		
	F. Untreated		
	G. Untreated		
Day 2 (a.m.)	A.		
	B.		
	C.		
	D.		
	E.		
	F.		
	G. Control		
Day 2 (p.m.)	A.		
	B.		
	C.		
	D.		
	E.		
	F.		
	G. Control		

Table 4.8   Watching bacteria grow (cont.)

Day	Container	Observations	Measurements (mm)
Day 3 (a.m.)	A.		
	B.		
	C.		
	D.		
	E.		
	F.		
	G. Control		
Day 3 (p.m.)	A.		
	B.		
	C.		
	D.		
	E.		
	F.		
	G. Control		

Table 4.9 Bacterial growth rates

Container/product	Diameters of colonies at end of day 1	Diameters of colonies at end of day 3	Difference (positive or negative)
A			
B			
C			
D			
E			
F			
G (Control)			

Step Six } **COMMUNICATE YOUR DATA IN AN APPROPRIATE MANNER.**
Because you are comparing the effectiveness of different antibacterial products over time, a line graph is appropriate (see p. 95). The x-axis should be labeled "Days." Label increments from day 1 to 3 and include a.m. and p.m. for days 2 and 3. The y-axis should be labeled "Diameter of bacterial colonies (mm)." Numbering the y-axis is a little tricky because you have both positive and negative values. This means you will begin numbering with a negative number. Find the range of your data from the lowest negative number to the highest positive number. Plot the twice-daily measurements for each product. Connect the dots. Use a different color pencil for each product. Include a key to identify the color for each product.

Include a table (see p. 95) listing the products you used and their active ingredients.

    0-7696-3429-X *Science Fair Projects: Volume 2*

Step Seven } **ANALYZE YOUR DATA TO DRAW CONCLUSIONS.** Based on your data, write a conclusion that summarizes your findings, states whether or not your hypothesis was correct, and identifies which type of antibacterial product was most effective at inhibiting the growth of bacteria. A large negative number indicates an effective product. If all of the products yielded about the same average amount of change, then you could conclude that they all worked about the same.

Step Eight } **EXPLAIN YOUR FINDINGS WITH AN INFERENCE.** Logically explain why the results of your experiment came out the way that they did, based on your research.

Alternatives and extensions

1. Conduct the same experiment using antibacterial liquid soaps and regular liquid soaps to determine if antibacterial soaps are more effective at inhibiting the rate of bacteria growth.

2. Collect and culture bacteria from a different source*, such as the door handle leading out of a restroom, and conduct the same type of experiment to determine whether the type of bacteria cultured changes the effectiveness of the antibacterial product.

* CAUTION: Use extreme care when culturing unknown species of bacteria. Use protective gloves and a mask when when working with the cultures. Keep the containers tightly sealed and dispose of the sealed containers in a thick plastic bag in an outdoor trash container at the end of the experiment.

    0-7696-3429-X *Science Fair Projects: Volume 2*

Bacterial growth rates

End of Day 1	Day 2—a.m.	Day 2—p.m.	Day 3—a.m.	Day 3—p.m.

Antibacterial products

Name of product	Active ingredient(s)

Preserving High-C

Step One }

MAKE AN OBSERVATION. You've probably heard about the importance of vitamin C in your diet. A vitamin is an organic nutrient that helps regulate the chemical reactions that convert food into energy and living tissue. Vitamin C is a water-soluble vitamin best known for its antioxidant properties. An *antioxidant* is a substance that prevents or slows oxidation. Many nutrients can be destroyed by oxidation. Vitamin C protects nutrients from oxidation by oxidizing itself. Human bodies do not produce or store vitamin C well, so vitamin C must be replenished from food or from dietary supplements.

Vitamin C is found naturally in many citrus fruits and vegetables. In addition, many foods are fortified with vitamin C, meaning that it has been added by the manufacturers. Whether natural or added, vitamin C oxidizes, or breaks itself down. The way food is stored or prepared can affect the amount of vitamin C food retains, which affects how much the body gets.

Step Two }

STATE THE PROBLEM AND POSE IT AS A RESEARCH QUESTION. Determine what effects different oxidizing agents have on the amount of vitamin C foods retain. In this investigation, you will use an indicator that reacts to the presence of vitamin C to compare how different oxidizing agents affect the amount of vitamin C retained in samples of freshly squeezed orange juice and other liquids.

> What is the effect you observe?

> What is the possible cause of the effect?

> How can it be posed as a research question?

Step Three }

CONDUCT YOUR RESEARCH. Investigate the terms *vitamins, vitamin C, nutrients, antioxidants,* and *oxidation.* Also investigate why vitamin C is important and what causes it to oxidize in foods. Write a summary of your findings to include in your presentation.

Step Four } **FORMULATE A HYPOTHESIS.** Identify the independent variable you will change in your experiment. Identify the dependent variable that will be affected by what you change. Write a testable hypothesis that predicts the relationship between the independent and dependent variables. Your hypothesis may be a positive statement predicting that none of the oxidizing agents will affect the amount of vitamin C retained in the samples, an independent statement predicting that a specific sample or oxidizing agent will affect the amount of vitamin C retained, or a negative statement predicting that none of the samples will retain their vitamin C when exposed to the various oxidizing agents.

Step Five } **DESIGN AND CONDUCT YOUR EXPERIMENT.**

A. Identify the variables you will keep the same during the experiment. Consider using the same testing method, cleaning the storage containers the same way, allowing the same amount of time for the reaction to occur, and introducing the oxidizing agents for the same amount of time.

B. Materials: 6 oranges, vitamin C tablets, unsweetened lemonade-flavored drink mix, a small saucepan, a microwave oven, a sunny area, sugar, distilled water, a mortar and pestle or plastic bag and metal spoon, 20 clean test tubes, a test-tube rack, a colander, a coffee filter, corn starch, 2% iodine solution (available from a pharmacist), a graduated cylinder, a dropper or pipette, a stove, 4 clean 2-liter soda bottles, 10 clean 8-oz. water bottles with tops, a timer, and a piece of white paper

C. Procedure

1. Prepare your indicator using the following steps.

    a. Measure 1 tablespoon of cornstarch in a small saucepan. Add enough distilled water to make a paste.

    b. Add 250 ml distilled water to the cornstarch paste.

    c. Heat the cornstarch solution on medium heat, stirring constantly. When the solution boils, turn down the heat and allow the solution to bubble gently for 5 minutes.

    d. Measure 75 ml distilled water and pour it into an 8-oz. water bottle.

    e. Use the dropper or pipette add 0.5 ml of the cooked starch solution to the water in the bottle.

    f. Slowly add drops of the iodine solution until the mixture turns a dark purple color.

    g. Put a top on the bottle and label it Indicator Solution.

    h. Store the bottle until ready to use.

CAUTION: Do not drink any of the solutions used in this experiment.

0-7696-3429-X *Science Fair Projects: Volume 2*

2. Dissolve the unsweetened drink mix in 2 liters of distilled water. Cap the bottle and shake until the mix dissolves. Label the bottle Fortified Drink Mix.

3. Cut and squeeze the 6 oranges and transfer the juice to a clean 2-liter bottle. Add distilled water to fill, cap it, and label it Fresh Juice.

4. Crush 3 vitamin-C tablets using the mortar and pestle or the plastic bag and metal spoon. Add the crushed tablets to 2 liters of distilled water. Cap and shake the bottle. Strain the contents through a colander lined with a coffee filter to remove any particles and pour the strained solution into a clean 2-liter bottle. Label the bottle Vitamin-Tablet Solution.

5. Place 3 test tubes in the test tube rack and place 5 drops of indicator solution in each.

6. Add 0.5 ml of the fortified drink mix to the first test tube.

7. Add 0.5 ml of the fresh juice to the second test tube.

8. Add 0.5 ml of the vitamin-tablet solution to the third test tube.

9. Wait 5 minutes. Place a piece of white paper behind the test tubes. Observe and rate the color of each solution in the Control column of table 4.11 (bottom of p. 99). These controls indicate the amount of vitamin C present in the freshly prepared (unoxidized) solutions.

Note to experimenter: Vitamin C causes the indicator solution to lose its purple color. This means that the lighter the solution is, the more vitamin C is in the solution. A complete color loss indicates a high vitamin C content.

10. Label the other 9 bottles as follows:

Fresh Juice—Sunlight	Drink Mix—Sunlight	Vitamin Tablet—Sunlight
Fresh Juice—Refrigerated	Drink Mix—Refrigerated	Vitamin Tablet—Refrigerated
Fresh Juice—Microwave	Drink Mix—Microwave	Vitamin Tablet—Microwave

11. Fill each bottle about half full of the solution on the label.

12. Place the bottles labeled Refrigerated together in the refrigerator and leave them for 4 days.

13. Place the bottles labeled Sunlight in direct sunlight where they will not be disturbed and leave them for 4 hours. Set a timer.

14. Microwave each of the bottles labeled Microwave for 30 seconds. Allow the solutions to cool.

15. When cool, test the microwaved solutions using steps 5–8. Use the rating scale (table 4.10, p. 99) to judge the color. Record the rating in table 4.11 in the Microwaved column.

16. While waiting for your solutions in direct sunlight, prepare and test the effects of sugar and direct heat as outlined in the next steps.

17. *Direct heat*—On a stove, in small clean saucepan, heat 1 cup of the fresh juice on medium until it starts to boil. Remove from heat and allow the juice to cool. Test the vitamin-C content using steps 5–8. Repeat the procedure for the unsweetened drink mix and the tablet solution. Thoroughly clean the saucepan each time. Use table 4.10 below to rate the color. Record the rating in table 4.11.

18. *Adding sugar*—Measure 1 cup of the fresh juice in a clean graduated cylinder. Add 6 tablespoons of sugar. Stir to dissolve the sugar. Allow the solution to sit for 30 minutes, and then test the vitamin C content using steps 5–8. Wash the measuring cup and cylinder. Repeat the procedure using the unsweetened drink mix and the vitamin-tablet solution. Use the rating scale and record the ratings in the observation table.

19. At the end of 4 hours, test each of the solutions in direct sunlight using steps 5–8. Use the rating scale and record your observations in the data table.

20. At the end of 4 days, test each of the refrigerated solutions using steps 5–8. Use the rating scale and record the rating in the table.

21. Dispose of remaining solutions and indicator by pouring them down the drain and flushing thoroughly with water.

D. Collect data.

Use tables 4.10 and 4.11 to rate and record your observations.

Table 4.10 Color scale

Color observed	Rating	Indications
Completely colorless	5	High presence of vitamin C in the solution
Almost completely colorless	4	Small loss of vitamin C in the solution
Half strength of original color	3	Loss of half the vitamin C in the solution
slightly less purple	2	Loss of most of the vitamin C in the solution
Full purple color	1	Loss of all the vitamin C in the solution

Table 4.11 Vitamin C observations

Solution tested	Control	Heated on stove	Sugar added	Microwaved	Direct sunlight	Refrigerated 4 days
Fresh juice						
Fortified drink mix						
Vitamin C tablet						

Step Six } **COMMUNICATE YOUR DATA IN AN APPROPRIATE MANNER.**
Because you are comparing the amount of vitamin C in each solution using a ranking scale, you can communicate your data using a multiple bar graph (see p. 101). To construct the graph, label the x-axis "Solution Tested." Write the types of solutions you tested in the middles of six bars.

Label the y-axis "Presence of Vitamin C." Number it from 1–5. Choose six colors to communicate the conditions tested (control, sunlight, microwaved, etc.). Use the colors for bars to show the vitamin-C values of each solution. Include a key and add the color scale (table 4.10, p. 99) below the graph. Title your graph.

Step Seven } **ANALYZE YOUR DATA TO DRAW CONCLUSIONS.** Based on your data, write a conclusion that summarizes your findings, states whether or not your hypothesis was correct, and identifies which condition produced the greatest loss of vitamin C in the solution. Also tell which condition retained the most vitamin C.

Step Eight } **EXPLAIN OUR FINDINGS WITH AN INFERENCE.** Logically explain why the results of your experiment came out the way that they did, based on your research.

Alternative and extension

Conduct the same type of test using fruits and vegetables that contain vitamin C to determine what effect different cooking and storage methods have on how much vitamin C is retained. Pulp the processed vegetables in a blender and strain them to test the juice. Avoid vegetables that have a high amount of color, as it will be hard to distinguish a color change. Consider using apples, grapefruits, cabbage, cauliflower, and turnips. In this investigation use raw fruits and vegetables as your control.

                    0-7696-3429-X *Science Fair Projects: Volume 2*

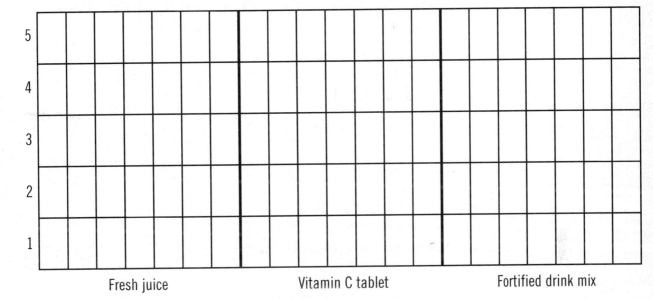

Presence of vitamin C (y-axis: 1, 2, 3, 4, 5)

Fresh juice   Vitamin C tablet   Fortified drink mix

Solution tested

Key	Control	Sugar added	Direct sunlight
	Heated on stove	Microwaved	Refrigerated

What a Way to Melt

Step One } **MAKE AN OBSERVATION.** What do you think is the best way to thaw food? To understand thawing, we need to understand energy transfers. Energy cannot be created or destroyed, but it can be converted (changed) and transferred. To thaw food, thermal energy is transferred from a warmer substance to a cooler substance. The warmer substance increases the molecular motion of the frozen food, causing the frozen water it in to change from a solid to a liquid. Some ways of thawing food allow bacteria to grow and can cause food poisoning. The method used to thaw food is crucial to both its quality and its safety.

Step Two } **STATE THE PROBLEM AND POSE IT AS A RESEARCH QUESTION.** Determine what methods of thawing solid water (ice) are fastest. In this investigation, you will freeze water and thaw it different ways.

> What is the effect you observe?

> What is the possible cause of the effect?

> How can it be posed as a research question?

Step Three } **CONDUCT YOUR RESEARCH.** Investigate the terms *conductivity*, *thermal energy*, *friction*, *temperature*, and *heat transfer*. Also investigate safety guidelines associated with thawing frozen food. Write a summary of your findings to include in your presentation

Step Four } **FORMULATE A HYPOTHESIS.** Identify the independent variable you will change in your experiment. Identify the dependent variable that will be affected by what you change. Write a testable hypothesis that predicts the relationship between the independent and dependent variables. Your hypothesis should predict which method thaws the water in the least amount of time and explain why you made this choice.

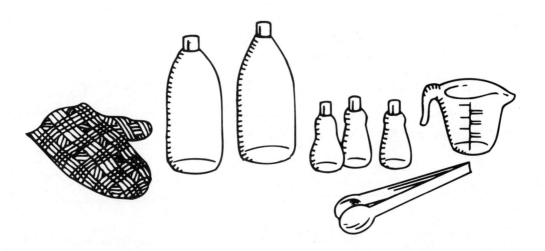

Step Five } **DESIGN AND CONDUCT YOUR EXPERIMENT.**

A. Identify the variables you will keep the same during the experiment. Consider using the same freezer, the same timer, the same water source, and the same amount of water in each bottle.

B. Materials: 12 clean 8-oz water bottles, a funnel, six 250-ml graduated cylinders, a freezer, a glass pie plate, tap water, a measuring cup, a dish pan, a sink, a refrigerator, an oven, tongs, an oven mitt, a timer, and a large pan (optional: you may want to color the water with food coloring to make it easier to measure).

C. Procedure

1. For each bottle, measure 3/4 cup of water, using the funnel to fill the water bottles.

2. Secure the caps on the bottles and place them in the freezer for 24 hours.

3. Make cards with the following labels. Place these cards under the graduated cylinders in which you will measure the amount of water thawed.

    - Boiling water
    - Oven
    - Running water

    - Countertop
    - Refrigerator
    - Pan of cold water

4. When you are ready to start the experiment, place a pan of water on the stove and bring it to a boil. Preheat the oven to 200°.

5. Fill a dishpan about 3/4 full of cold tapwater and set it on the counter.

6. When the boiling water and the oven are ready, remove 6 of your frozen bottles from the freezer at the same time.

7. Immediately place the bottles in the following places:

    - pan of boiling water (burner off)
    - glass pie pan in oven—put bottle and pie plate in at the same time
    - refrigerator
    - dish pan of cold water
    - sink under cold running water
    - countertop

8. Set the timer. Monitor the frozen water at 1-minute intervals.

CAUTION: Use tongs to remove the bottle from the pan of hot water and use an oven mitt to remove the bottle from the oven.

9. When all of the ice in one bottle is completely thawed, stop the timer and remove the other bottles. Record the times and thawing methods in the space provided in table 5.1 on page 104.

10. Pour the thawed water from each bottle into the correctly labeled graduated cylinder. Record the measurements in table 5.1.

11. Repeat the experiment (steps 4–9) and find the average amount of water thawed by adding the two measurements together and dividing by two.

D. Collect Data.

Which method melted the ice fastest?

Time to thaw (trial 1)_____ Method used _____

Time to thaw (trial 2)_____ Method used _____

Table 5.1 Thawing ice results

Method	Amount of water trial 1	Amount of water trial 2	Total water thawed	÷ 2	Avg. water thawed
Under running water				÷ 2	
In pan of cold water				÷ 2	
In pan of boiling water				÷ 2	
In oven at 200° F				÷ 2	
In the refrigerator				÷ 2	
On the counter at room temp.				÷ 2	

Step Six }

COMMUNICATE YOUR DATA IN AN APPROPRIATE MANNER.

Because you are comparing amounts of water thawed, it is best to use a multiple bar graph (see p. 106). Label the x-axis "Method used to thaw." Each method will require three bars, so write the method under the bars. Label the y-axis "Amount of water thawed (ml)." Number the axis by tens. After you add labels and numbers to the graph, use colored pencils to communicate your data—one color for trial 1, one for trial 2, and one for the average of the two trials. Include a key and a title.

0-7696-3429-X *Science Fair Projects: Volume 2*

Step Seven } **ANALYZE YOUR DATA TO DRAW CONCLUSIONS.** Based on your data, write a conclusion that summarizes your findings, states whether or not your hypothesis was correct, and identifies which methods were most and least effective at thawing water.

Step Eight } **EXPLAIN YOUR RESULTS WITH AN INFERENCE.** Logically explain why the results of your experiment came out the way that they did, based on your research.

Alternatives and extensions

1. Sometimes we want a substance to stay frozen, so, we use insulators to prevent or slow the transfer of thermal energy. Conduct an experiment to determine what effect different insulating materials have on the length of time a frozen substance stays frozen. Use frozen water bottles and insulate them with different materials (foam, newspaper, felt, etc.). Allow them to sit in the same place for a determined length of time. When the time is up, use a graduated cylinder to measure the amount of liquid in each container. Set your graph up to show the relationship between the material used to insulate the containers and the amount of water thawed.

2. There is a theory that water boiled and cooled freezes faster than cold water. Determine if this is true by timing how long it takes different trays of water to freeze. You will need a thermometer, a heating and cooling source, a timer, a lot of freezer space, and several ice cube trays. Use a thermometer to measure the temperature. Label the ice cube trays and fill them half full. Place the trays in the freezer. Use a timer and monitor the status of the cubes every five minutes. Record the time it takes each tray to completely freeze. Repeat the experiment and find the average time. Use a multiple line graph to communicate your data.

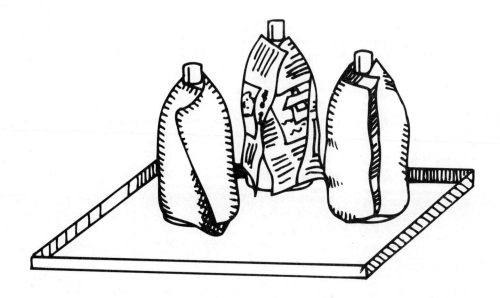

                    0-7696-3429-X *Science Fair Projects: Volume 2*

0-7696-3429-X *Science Fair Projects: Volume 2*

Take Down, Break Down, You're Busted

Step One } **MAKE AN OBSERVATION.** Proteins are complex molecules made up of chains of amino acids and other materials. Amino acids are made up of carbon, oxygen, nitrogen, and hydrogen. There are twenty amino acids in the proteins of living organisms. These twenty combine to form many different proteins. The type of protein formed depends on the needs of the organism. The human body uses proteins to grow and to repair itself and to protect itself from disease.

Human bodies use digestive enzymes to break apart the chains of amino acids in the protein in foods. The amino acids are then rebuilt as the proteins the body can use. Enzymes are molecules that speed up a chemical reaction—such as digesting food. Thousands of enzymes are found naturally in all living organisms. Enzymes are classified in three main types.

Type of enzyme	Where found and what they do
Metabolic	Run body systems by speeding up chemical reactions in cells
Digestive	Assist in digestion—assimilating, using, and eliminating food
Food	Naturally present in raw foods—provide an external source of digestive enzymes

Each type of enzyme performs a specific job. Enzymes regulate most of the chemical reactions that occur in living things. They enable the body's systems to do their work. Some enzymes help make new substances in the body and others help break down unwanted substances. Enzymes not only speed up reactions, they also make sure that the reactions happen in the right place and at the right time. The way an enzyme works is affected by temperature, pH, and pressure.

Step Two } **STATE THE PROBLEM AND POSE IT AS A RESEARCH QUESTION.** Determine what effect temperature has on an enzyme's ability to break down protein. In this investigation, you will explore how different temperatures of enzymes affect the ability of gelatin samples (made of pure protein) to thicken and gel. This is evidence of how well an enzyme works.

> What is the effect you observe?

> What is the possible cause of the effect?

> How can it be posed as a research question?

Step Three } **CONDUCT YOUR RESEARCH.** Investigate the terms *enzyme, protein, amino acids, catalyst, chemical reaction,* and *digestion.* Investigate how enzymes in food are affected by temperature, pH, and pressure. Write a summary of your findings to include in your presentation.

Step Four } **FORMULATE A HYPOTHESIS.** Identify the independent variable you will change in your experiment. Identify the dependent variable that will be affected by what you change. Write a testable hypothesis that predicts the relationship between the independent and dependent variables. Your hypothesis may predict that temperature does not affect on the way enzymes work. Or you may predict that enzymes will work in a specific range of temperatures.

Step Five } **DESIGN AND CONDUCT YOUR EXPERIMENT.**

A. Identify the variables you will keep the same during the experiment. Consider making enzyme solutions using the same source of water, using the same brand of gelatin, and allowing the samples to gel under the same conditions for the same amount of time.

B. Materials: 4 packets unflavored gelatin, distilled water, 1 can thawed pineapple juice concentrate, meat tenderizer, Celsius thermometer, large measuring cup, mixing spoon, water, 13 clean pipettes, 39 small plastic cups, permanent marker, plastic wrap, coffee stirrers, and a saucepan

C. Procedure

1. Mix 1 tablespoon of meat tenderizer in 1 cup of warm water and stir until dissolved.

2. Divide the tenderizer solution equally into 6 small plastic cups. Label the cups to indicate what is in them and where they will rest for the next 15 minutes. Change the temperature of each solution by placing a cup in each of the following places:

   - in the freezer for 15 minutes
   - in a container of very hot water for 15 minutes.
   - in a container of ice water for 15 minutes.
   - on the counter for 15 minutes.
   - in the refrigerator for 15 minutes.
   - in the microwave, heated for 30 seconds (at the end the 15 minutes)

3. Repeat step 2 using thawed pineapple juice concentrate in place of the meat tenderizer solution.

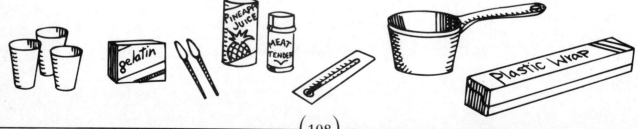

4. While you wait for your enzymes to change temperature, prepare 2 packets of gelatin in a large measuring cup using only half the recommended boiling and cold water amounts in the package directions. Stir well with a spoon until all of the gelatin dissolves. Set the mixture aside.

5. When steps 2 and 3 are complete, measure the temperature of the enzyme in each cup and record it in the second column of table 5.2 (p. 110). Your temperatures should range from 0 to 100°C.

6. Use a clean pipette for each cup to transfer 5 ml of the enzyme from each cup to a new plastic cup. Label the new cups with a letter from table 5.2 to indicate the temperature and type of enzyme.

7. Add the gelatin mixture to each new cup until it is 1/3 full. Fill 2 additional (empty) cups 1/3 full of the gelatin mixture and label these cups Control.

8. Cover all the cups with plastic wrap and place them in a cool place (30–35°C) where they will not be disturbed for at least 12 hours.

9. Check how well the samples have gelled after 12 hours by trying to stir them with a coffee stirrer. Use a clean stirrer for each sample. Write your observations in table 5.2.

D. Collect Data.
Use the scale on page 112 to rate the condition of each sample. Record the rating in table 5.2 (p. 110). Repeat the experiment. Average the ratings for both trials.

Note to experimenter: Gelatin is pure protein made from dehydrated animal collagen. By adding water, you hydrolyze (or rehydrate) its molecules, allowing its amino acids to form protein chains as it cools. Enzymes can prevent protein chains from forming by digesting the protein, resulting in a liquid gelatin mixture. The gelatin that solidified was not affected by the enzyme.

0-7696-3429-X *Science Fair Projects: Volume 2*

Table 5.2   How well did it gel?

Enzyme used	Temperature C°	Observations at end of 12 hours	Rate: 0–4	Average
Control: No enzyme added	Trial 1 n/a			
	Trial 2 n/a			
A. Tenderizer in freezer	Trial 1			
	Trial 2			
B. Tenderizer in hot water	Trial 1			
	Trial 2			
C. Tenderizer in ice water	Trial 1			
	Trial 2			
D. Tenderizer at room temp.	Trial 1			
	Trial 2			
E. Tenderizer in refrigerator	Trial 1			
	Trial 2			
F. Tenderizer microwaved	Trial 1			
	Trial 2			
G. Pineapple in freezer	Trial 1			
	Trial 2			
H. Pineapple in hot water	Trial 1			
	Trial 2			
I. Pineapple in ice water	Trial 1			
	Trial 2			
J. Pineapple at room temp.	Trial 1			
	Trial 2			
K. Pineapple in refrigerator	Trial 1			
	Trial 2			
L. Pineapple microwaved	Trial 1			
	Trial 2			

Published by Milestone. Copyright protected.

0-7696-3429-X *Science Fair Projects: Volume 2*

Step Six }

COMMUNICATE YOUR DATA IN AN APPROPRIATE MANNER. Because the temperature of the solutions used is a type of continuous data, use a double line graph (p. 112) to communicate the findings. Label the *x*-axis "Temperature of Enzyme Solution (°C)." Number this axis by tens from 0 to 100. The *y*-axis should be labeled "Gelatin Rating" and numbered 0 to 4. Use one color for the six meat tenderizer solutions and plot the averages of both trials. Use a second color to plot the averaged data for the pineapple juice samples. Include a key and a title. Include the scale used to rate the gelatin samples in your presentation.

Step Seven }

ANALYZE YOUR DATA TO DRAW CONCLUSIONS. Based on your data, write a conclusion that summarizes your findings, states whether or not your hypothesis was correct, and identifies which temperatures affected the enzyme's ability to break down proteins. If the gelatin gelled, the enzyme was not effective. If the gelatin remained liquid, the protein it contained was digested by the enzyme.

Step Eight }

EXPLAIN YOUR FINDINGS WITH AN INFERENCE. Logically explain why the results of your experiment came out the way that they did, based on your research. Include how this experiment relates to the preservation of enzymes naturally found in different types of food.

Alternatives and extensions

1. Enzymes occur in many foods. Conduct the same type of experiment using juices from different foods (apples, papayas, oranges, kiwis, grapefruits, grapes, etc.). Puree and strain the foods or use thawed frozen concentrates to determine which contain enzymes that digest proteins.

2. Conduct an experiment to determine what effect pH has on an enzyme's ability to break down protein. Use thawed pineapple juice or the meat tenderizer solution, but change its pH by altering the solution in two ways: use a 5% vinegar acidic solution or mix a basic solution by adding two tablespoons of baking soda to one cup of warm water and stir. Use the acid and base solutions to mix the following concentrations of enzyme solutions.

Table 5.3

Solution concentration	Enzyme amount (ml)	Amount of acid or base (ml)
75%	15	5
50%	10	10
25%	5	10
10%	1	10l

Label the concentrations. Follow the procedure on pages 108–109 to determine if changing the pH affects how well the enzyme breaks down protein.

 0-7696-3429-X *Science Fair Projects: Volume 2*

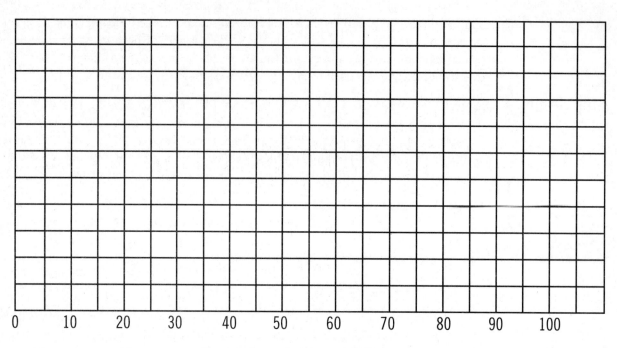

Temperature of enzyme solution

Table 5.4   Gelatin rating scale

Gelatin's condition	Rate	Indications
Completely firm/ no liquid	0	Enzyme did not digest any protein in the gelatin sample.
Almost completely firm/ very little liquid	1	Enzyme partially digested protein in the gelatin sample.
half gelled, half liquid	2	Enzyme digested half of the protein in the gelatin sample.
partially gelled, mostly liquid	3	Enzyme digested most of the protein in the gelatin sample.
No gel, all liquid	4	Enzyme completely digested the protein in the gelatin sample.

It's Alive!

Step One }

MAKE AN OBSERVATION. Scientists can determine when something died by looking at what is living in and on the dead organism. Hundreds of years ago, people observed living things in and around dead things and concluded that living organisms came from dead organisms. This theory, known as spontaneous generation, was put to the test in the 1600s by Italian physician Francisco Redi. Redi conducted an experiment by placing rotting meat in three sets of jars. One set of jars was left open, allowing oxygen to get in, another set was sealed to prevent the intake of oxygen, and the third set was covered with a mesh screen. Redi observed that maggots, the larval stage of many carrion flies, appeared in the open jars and the jars covered with a screen. Maggots did not appear on the meat in the sealed jars. Redi concluded that the maggots did not come from the meat but from the air surrounding the meat, thereby disproving the theory of spontaneous generation. Today we know that insects play an important role in nature as they break down and recycle the nutrients in dead organisms. By studying different carrion insects (insects that feed on dead animals), scientists have developed an insect clock they can use to determine an approximate time of death of an organism.

Step Two }

STATE THE PROBLEM AND POSE IT AS A RESEARCH QUESTION. Determine what effect different environmental conditions have on the growth and development of carrion insects. In this investigation, you will attempt to raise carrion flies to develop an insect clock based on your observations.

> What is the effect you observe?

> What is the possible cause of the effect?

> How can it be posed as a research question?

  0-7696-3429-X *Science Fair Projects: Volume 2*

Step Three } **CONDUCT YOUR RESEARCH.** Investigate the terms *carrion insects, decay, forensic entomology,* and *spontaneous generation.* Investigate and identify different species of carrion insects as to their life cycles and natural habitats. Write a summary of your findings to include in your presentation.

Step Four } **FORMULATE A HYPOTHESIS.** Identify the independent variable you will change in your experiment. Identify the dependent variable that will be affected by what you change. Write a testable hypothesis that predicts the relationship between the independent and dependent variables. Your hypothesis may predict that carrion flies will develop faster under a specific condition or that the environmental condition will not affect the rate at which carrion flies develop.

Step Five } **DESIGN AND CONDUCT YOUR EXPERIMENT.**

A. Identify the variables you will keep the same during the experiment. Consider using the same amount and kind of raw liver, placing the liver in the same type of containers, and leaving the liver in its location for the same amount of time.

B. Materials: 3 pieces of raw liver, waxed paper, small-gauge wire fencing, wire cutters, 3 sturdy shoe boxes, a pair of scissors, a hand lens, tweezers, 4 jars with lids, a journal, a heavy-duty freezer bag, rubbing alcohol, duct tape, staking nails, a hammer, a ruler (mm), a trash bag, and a microscope

C. Procedure

1. Cut a large opening in the lid of each shoe box.

2. Use the wire cutters to cut a piece of fencing large enough to cover the openings in the lids. Use duct tape to secure the fencing inside the lids.

3. Cover the inside of each shoe box with waxed paper.

4. Place a piece of liver in the bottom of each of your boxes, put on the lids, and secure them with duct tape.

5. Choose a sunny place for one box. Use your staking nails to secure the box.

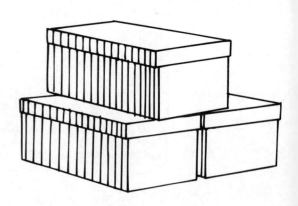

6. Place another box in a shady place. Use your staking nails to secure that box.

7. Place the third box in your garage in an area where it will not be disturbed for 15 days.

8. Wait 24 hours. Fill 3 jars with rubbing alcohol. Label them "Garage," "Sunny place," and "Shady place."

9. Carry a jar, tweezers, and a hand lens to each location and remove the box lid. Use the hand lens to observe the piece of meat. If you see any eggs on the meat, count them and record the number in a journal. Use the tweezers to carefully collect several samples of eggs, larva, etc. Place the samples in the jar of alcohol and replace the lids on the box and on the jar. Take your specimen jars inside.

CAUTION: Wash your hands thoroughly with soap and warm water after collecting and working with specimens from the liver. Sterilize the tweezers by soaking them in rubbing alcohol for 30 minutes in a lidded container after each use.

10. Use a microscope or a hand lens. Measure the specimens and record measurements in table 5.5 (p. 116). Sketch your specimens in your journal. Label your sketches with the day number and the location from which you took the specimens.

11. Repeat steps 9 and 10 daily for the next 14 days. If adult insects appear, hang sticky fly strips above the boxes to capture them. Use tweezers to remove them from the strips. Place them in your specimen jars.

12. Complete your data table. Dispose of the liver and boxes in a heavy trash bag.

D. Collect Data. Use the record sheet on page 116.

0-7696-3429-X *Science Fair Projects: Volume 2*

INVESTIGATING THE NATURAL WORLD

Table 5.5 Record of carrion insect growth

Day and location	Stage(s) observed (egg, larva, pupa, adult)	Measurements of 3 or more specimens (mm)	Sketches made? (yes or no)
Day 1 Sunny place			
Day 1 Shady place			
Day 1 Garage			
Day 2 Sunny place			
Day 2 Shady place			
Day 2 Garage			
Day 3 Sunny place			
Day 3 Shady place			
Day 3 Garage			
Day 4 Sunny place			
Day 4 Shady place			
Day 4 Garage			
Day 5 Sunny place			
Day 5 Shady place			
Day 5 Garage			
Day 6 Sunny place			
Day 6 Shady place			
Day 6 Garage			
Day 7 Sunny place			
Day 7 Shady place			
Day 7 Garage			
Day 8 Sunny place			
Day 8 Shady place			
Day 8 Garage			
Day 9 Sunny place			
Day 9 Shady place			
Day 9 Garage			
Day 10 Sunny place			
Day 10 Shady place			
Day 10 Garage			
Day 11 Sunny place			
Day 11 Shady place			
Day 11 Garage			
Day 12 Sunny place			
Day 12 Shady place			
Day 12 Garage			
Day 13 Sunny place			
Day 13 Shady place			
Day 13 Garage			
Day 14 Sunny place			
Day 14 Shady place			
Day 14 Garage			
Day 15 Sunny place			
Day 15 Shady place			
Day 15 Garage			

0-7696-3429-X *Science Fair Projects: Volume 2*

Step Six } **COMMUNICATE YOUR DATA IN AN APPROPRIATE MANNER.** Because you record the number of days spent in each stage, use a multiple bar graph (below). Label the *x*-axis "Stage of carrion insect development." Label the *y*-axis "Number of days" and number it 0 to 15. Use a different color pencil to show the data for each location. Your bars will start on the day you first observe each stage and end on the day you first observe the next stage of development. Add a key to communicate which color represents each location and add a title to the graph. Also include your observation table and your journal in your presentation.

Step Seven } **ANALYZE YOUR DATA TO DRAW CONCLUSIONS.** Based on your data, write a conclusion that summarizes your findings, states whether or not your hypothesis was correct, and identifies the length of time it took carrion flies to develop under each of the environmental conditions tested. Also report any location where flies did not develop.

Step Eight } **EXPLAIN YOUR FINDINGS WITH AN INFERENCE.** Logically explain why the results of your experiment came out the way they did, based on your research.

Alternatives and extensions

1. Conduct the same experiment using other types of meat and the same locations to determine if the type of meat has an effect on the rate at which carrion insects grow and develop.

2. Place samples of liver treated with salt and other preserving agents in the same locations to determine what effect preserving agents have on the rate at which carrion insects develop and grow.

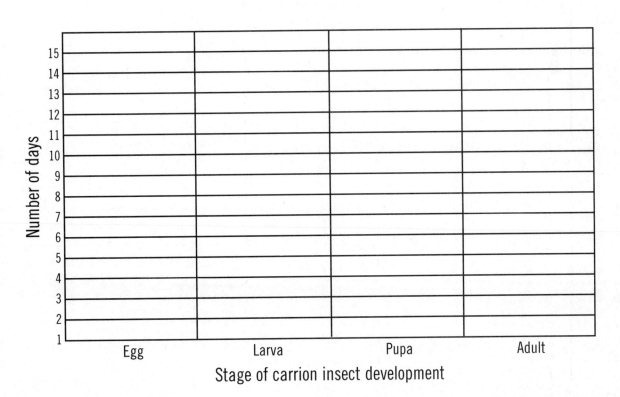

Don't Leaven Me Out

Step One }

MAKE AN OBSERVATION. Some recipes call for baking soda or baking powder. These ingredients are leavening agents. Leavening agents increase the volume of a substance, usually a baked good. The type of leavening agent used depends on several factors—the product, the amount of lift needed, and the other ingredients used.

Leavening agents work in a variety of ways. Some, like egg whites, form a matrix that traps air. When heated, the trapped air bubbles expand, causing the batter to rise. Others liberate carbon dioxide through a chemical reaction. As the gas is released, the batter rises. For example, yeast metabolizes in bread and releases CO_2 that causes the bread to rise. Baking soda, a base, chemically reacts with a proton donor acid to liberate CO_2 and water. Baking powder works on the same principle as baking soda, but it already has an acid and a base ready to react when water is added.

Step Two }

STATE THE PROBLEM AND POSE IT AS A RESEARCH QUESTION. Determine what effect different amounts of different leavening agents have on the quality of a baked good. In this investigation, you will modify the leavening agents used in a cupcake recipe to determine which agent or combination of agents produces the best cupcakes.

> What is the effect you observe?

> What is the possible cause of the effect?

> How can it be posed as a research question?

Step Three }

CONDUCT YOUR RESEARCH. Investigate the terms *leavening agent*, *chemical reaction*, *metabolize*, *acids*, and *bases*. Also investigate how different leavening agents work. Write a summary of your findings to include in your presentation.

Step Four }

FORMULATE A HYPOTHESIS. Identify the independent variable you will change in your experiment. Identify the dependent variable that will be affected by what you change. Write a testable hypothesis that predicts the relationship between the independent and dependent variables. Your hypothesis may predict that a particular leavening agent or combination of leavening agents will produce the best cupcakes or that the type of leavening agent used will have no effect on the quality of the cupcakes.

Step Five } **DESIGN AND CONDUCT YOUR EXPERIMENT.**

A. Identify the variables you will keep the same during the experiment. Consider using the same recipe, the same nonleavening ingredients, the same oven, and observing the same characteristics for each batch of cupcakes.

B. Materials: flour, sugar, butter, eggs, milk, vanilla, baking soda, baking powder, yeast, measuring cup, measuring spoons, 2 mixing bowls, wooden spoon, 32 cupcake liners, a permanent marker, 1 six-holed cupcake pan, and an oven

C. Procedure

1. Label cupcake liners with the leavening agents shown below. You will make 4 cupcakes with each leavening agent.

   A. 2 tsp. baking powder

   B. 1 tsp. baking soda + 1/2 tsp. vinegar

   C. 2 tsp. baking soda

   D. 1 tsp. baking soda + 1 tsp. baking powder

   E. 1 tsp. dry yeast

   F. 1 whipped egg white

   G. No leavening agent (control)

2. Preheat oven to 350°F. Line the muffin tin with 4 cupcake liners for the first leavening agent. Put 1/8 cup water in the empty cups of the pan.

3. Follow the recipe below to make the batter for 4 cupcakes.

Cupcake Recipe

   a. Measure 1/2 cup + 1 tablespoon + 1 teaspoon of flour into a mixing bowl.

   b. In another bowl, cream 1/2 cup sugar with 1/2 cup butter until smooth.

   c. Add 1/2 cup of milk and 1 egg to the creamed sugar and butter. Mix well with a wooden spoon.

   d. Add test leavening agent to the flour. Mix the dry ingredients with the moist ingredients using a wooden spoon until the batter is smooth. Do not overmix.

   e. Spoon the batter into the cupcake liners until the liners are 2/3 full.

   f. Bake the cupcakes for 15 minutes.

   g. Remove the cupcakes from the oven and let them cool on a wire rack.

D. Collect Data.
After the cupcakes cool, fill in table 5.6 (p. 120). Repeat the procedure with the other 5 leavening agents and with no leavening. Complete your observation table.

 0-7696-3429-X *Science Fair Projects: Volume 2*

Table 5.6   Rating leavening agents in cupcakes

Characteristic	A. 2 tsp. baking powder	B. 1 tsp. baking soda + 1 tsp. vinegar	C. 2 tsp. baking soda	D. 1 tsp. baking soda + 1 tsp. baking powder	E. 1 tsp. dry yeast	F. 1 whipped egg white	G. No agent added
Height in center (cm)							
Outside color							
Appearance of top of cake							
Inside color							
Texture							
Flavor							
Size and uniformity of bubbles							
Distinguishing characteristics							
Rank in order of preference 1–7*							

*1 = most likely to eat and 7 = least likely to eat

0-7696-3429-X *Science Fair Projects: Volume 2*

Step Six } **COMMUNICATE YOUR DATA IN AN APPROPRIATE MANNER.** Because your data is based on observations, include your observation table in your presentation.

Step Seven } **ANALYZE YOUR DATA TO DRAW CONCLUSIONS.** Based on your data, write a conclusion that summarizes your findings, states whether or not your hypothesis was correct, and identifies the leavening agents that produced the least and most desirable cupcakes.

Step Eight } **EXPLAIN YOUR FINDINGS WITH AN INFERENCE.** Logically explain why the results of your experiment came out as they did, based on your research. Include how this experiment relates to food chemistry and why different recipes call for different leavening agents.

Alternatives and extensions

1. Choose a different recipe, such as one for cookies, and follow the same procedure to determine what effect different leavening agents have on how a cookie tastes.

2. Expose baking powder to different conditions and use each sample in the recipe for cupcakes to determine what effect different conditions have on how well your cupcakes turn out. To conduct this test, put several tablespoons of baking powder in several cups. Place the cups in different places, such as outside on a humid day, in the refrigerator, in direct sunlight, in the dark, and in a sealed bag. Variables to control include using the same recipe, using the same nonleavening ingredients, exposing the baking powder to different conditions for the same amount of time, and observing and testing the same characteristics.

In a science fair, the way a project is presented is extremely important. A great experiment may not receive the recognition it deserves because it appears sloppy or has critical elements missing in the presentation. In other words, neatness counts! Above all, be certain that you closely follow the criteria your teacher gives for your project.

Here are suggestions for effectively displaying and presenting a science fair experiment.

Display Backboard

The display backboard is what people see first. It establishes the professionalism of your efforts and advertises your project. It must be well designed and constructed for maximum visual effect. Many companies offer prepackaged display boards designed for science fairs.

First, consider size when choosing a display backboard. Contact the science fair coordinator at your school to check the size limitations. The typical size for a display is 3' x 3'.

Next, consider the material you will use to construct your backboard. You can use plywood, peg board, foam board, or other sturdy materials. Below is one successful design for a backboard. This design does not require a separate stand. And it closes flat for safe and easy travel.

After the backboard is cut or purchased, paint it or cover it in a solid-color fabric.

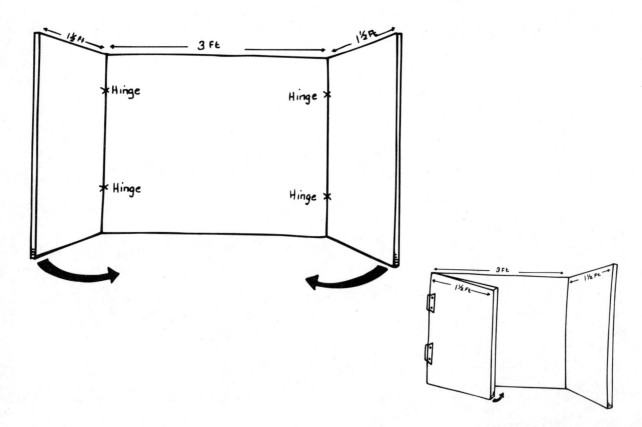

Display Format

Now determine what goes on the backboard. Include all the required information in an appealing format that is easy to read. Use these guidelines for what to include.

1. *Your research question.* Place the question at the top of the display in large letters. The question introduces your experiment and states what you are trying to find out.

2. *The purpose or problem you are researching.* List your reasons for pursuing the project and identify what you hoped to learn from the experiment. Make your statement clear and concise.

3. *Your hypothesis.* State what effect you predict the independent variable will have on the dependent variable. It is written as an "if/then" statement.

4. *Identify variables.* List the independent, dependent, and controlled variables.

5. *Materials.* List all of the materials you used to conduct the experiment.

6. *Your procedure.* Include a step-by-step explanation of how you conducted the experiment. Write clearly so that someone else could repeat your experiment.

7. *Data collected during the experiment.* Display your data tables and graph. Be sure your labels and titles communicate clearly.

8. *Your conclusion.* Make this is a concise statement telling whether your hypothesis was correct or not and summarizing your data.

9. *Your inference.* Make a concise statement that explains why your experiment turned out the way it did.

For neatness, type your materials. Use a font large enough to read easily. You may mount sections on colored papers to make your display more attractive. Try laying out your materials in several different ways before attaching them to the board.

 0-7696-3429-X *Science Fair Projects: Volume 2*

Optional Items for Your Display

1. *Pictures.* Photographs taken during your experiment illustrate the project and add authenticity to your work.

2. *Apparatus.* If the apparatus used in the experiment is small, display it in front of the backboard. For example, place a can of baking powder and a box of baking soda in front of the backboard for the experiment "Don't Leaven Me Out." Or set the water testing strips used in "Water Way To Treat Me" in front of the display board. If the apparatus is too large or dangerous to display, include some photographs of it.

The Report

Your written report summarizes everything you did to investigate and answer your research question. It should contain all the information you collected or learned during the investigation.

Neatly type or handwrite the report and put it in an attractive binder or folder. The written report should include the following:

1. *Title page.* Include the research question or title of the project, and the experimenter's name and grade level.

2. *Table of contents.* List the different parts of the project and their page numbers in the report.

3. *Statement of purpose or problem investigated.* This two- or three- sentence statement explains why you chose the topic. Include the cause and effect associated with the topic.

4. *Research.* Include all the background information you collected and researched through books, the Internet, or a professional in the field. Write the information in your words. Do not copy from the Internet or another source.

5. *Hypothesis.* This if/then statement (based on research) predicts what effect you believe the independent variable will have on the dependent variable.

6. *Materials.* List all the supplies and specific quantities of materials you used in the project.

7. *Procedure.* Describe the steps you followed in a numbered list. Your goal is to tell the reader how to conduct the same experiment.

8. *Observations and results.* Outline what you learned from the experiment. Include graphs, charts, and data tables in this section.

9. *Conclusion.* Briefly analyze and summarize the data or observations you made during the experiment. Also state whether your hypothesis was correct or incorrect.

10. *Inference.* Briefly explain why the experiment turned out the way that it did. You can also guide future experimenters by pointing out what you would do differently if you were to repeat the experiment.

11. *Timeline.* Outline the way you managed your time preparing for the science fair. Let the reader know how long the experiment would take to replicate.

12. *Bibliography.* List all the resources and reference materials you used during the investigation. List sources in alphabetical order using the standard format.

The Completed Project

When complete, your science fair project should be neat and thorough. You should display it in an organized way so judges can find information quickly and easily. The example below is a completed project set up for viewing by judges and others at the science fair.

Most important, enjoy the science fair!

0-7696-3429-X *Science Fair Projects: Volume 2*

JUDGING OR GRADING RUBRIC

Display Backboard	Score

Creativity (*25 points*) _____
- ○ Materials are presented in an imaginative way.
- ○ Distinctive approach to problem solving.
- ○ Original project and/or display.
- ○ New and interesting information included.
- ○ Student has shown inventiveness.
- ○ Visuals complement the information.

Scientific Thought (30 points) _____
- ○ Experiment is designed to answer research question.
- ○ Research question is clearly stated.
- ○ Variables are correctly identified.
- ○ Hypothesis is testable.
- ○ Scientific literature is cited.
- ○ Data collected is communicated in correct format.
- ○ Conclusion statement reflects data.
- ○ Inference explains experimental results.
- ○ Steps of the scientific method were followed.
- ○ Project notebook is sufficiently detailed and relates well to the investigation.
- ○ Procedure is clearly outlined and designed to answer research question.
- ○ Amount of data collected is commensurate with the project.
- ○ Student shows a clear understanding of the facts and theories related to his/her project.

Thoroughness (*15 points*) _____
- ○ Project is complete.
- ○ Research question was adequately answered or pursued.
- ○ Notes are complete.
- ○ Project includes a display backboard, visuals, and a written report.
- ○ Project tells a complete story.
- ○ Research included relates well to research question.
- ○ Cause and effect relationship is established through the research question.
- ○ Conclusion is supported by the results of the experiment.
- ○ Inference clearly explains the results of the experiment.

Display Backboard	Score

Clarity (*15 points*) _____
- ○ Titles and written information is legible and easy to read
- ○ Data is presented clearly.
- ○ Average person can understand the project.
- ○ Written material is well prepared.
- ○ Project is self-explanatory.
- ○ Procedure is clear and concise enough to replicate.
- ○ Drawings, diagrams, and pictures are neat and labeled.
- ○ Presentation is logical and sequential.
- ○ Every piece of material included in presentation is important to the display.
- ○ Conclusions and inferences are clearly stated.

Skill (*15 points*) _____
- ○ Project represents the student's own work.
- ○ Project displays quality construction.
- ○ Project is artistically pleasing and well put together.
- ○ Project indicates extensive planning and wise use of time.
- ○ Display does not contain any dangerous or unsuitable materials.
- ○ Project indicates that student understands the information.
- ○ Equipment used is within the student's level of understanding or expertise.

Total for Display (*100 points*) _____

| Written Report | Score | Written Report | Score |

Title page (*2 points*) _____

○ Page contains research question, student's name and grade level.

Table of Contents (*5 points*) _____

○ All parts are listed.

○ Parts are listed in order.

○ Page numbers are correct.

Statement of Purpose or Problem (*10 points*) _____

○ Poses a question that can be investigated.

○ Relates the question through cause and effect.

○ Explains why student chose topic.

Research (*15 points*) _____

○ Research presented pertains to topic investigated.

○ Research is written in student's own words.

○ Research is thorough.

○ Research is clearly presented and documented.

Hypothesis (*5 points*) _____

○ Hypothesis shows a relationship between the independent and dependent variables.

○ Hypothesis is testable.

○ Hypothesis is written as an if/then statement.

○ Hypothesis is scientifically sound.

Materials (*5 points*) _____

○ All materials used are listed.

○ Amounts used are indicated.

Procedure (*10 points*) _____

○ Controlled variables are identified.

○ Procedure is clearly written using a step-by-step format.

○ Procedure is scientifically sound to test the hypothesis.

○ Procedure is presented in a logical, sequential manner.

○ Procedure could be replicated.

Observations, Data Tables, and Graphs (*15 points*) _____

○ Data tables are clearly labeled and titled.

○ Data relates to the experiment.

○ Observations relate well to the experiment.

○ Observations and data support what was done during the experiment.

○ Observations and data were reported in the appropriate manner.

○ An appropriate graph was used to communicate data.

○ Graphs are clearly labeled and titled.

Conclusion and Inferences (*15 points*) _____

○ Conclusion states whether the hypothesis was proved or disproved.

○ Conclusion is supported by data.

○ Conclusion answers the research question.

○ Inference clearly explains the data.

○ Inference indicates what the student would change if redoing the experiment.

Bibliography (*8 points*) _____

○ Bibliography is complete and in alphabetical order.

○ Bibliography is presented in correct format.

Timeline (*10 points*) _____

○ Timeline indicates good use of time.

○ Timeline is complete.

○ Timeline is well organized.

Total for Written Report (*100 points*) _____

Total for Project (*200 points*) _____

Comments: _____
_____
_____
_____
_____

Drinking water standards as adopted by the EPA Safe Drinking Water Act

Pollutant	Maximum Contaminant Level mg/L
Alpha Particle activity (gross)	15 pCi/L
Arsenic	0.01
Bacteria	4/100ml
Barium	2.00
Benzene (organic)	0.005
Beta particle and photon radioactivity	4 mrem/yr
Cadmium	0.005
Carbon tetrachloride (organic)	0.005
Chloride	250.0
Color (platinum-cobalt scale)	15 units
Coliform	5%
Chromium (haxavalent)	0.001
Copper	1.3
Cyanide	0.02
1,1 dichloroethylene (organic)	0.007
1,2 dichloroethylene (organic)	0.005
Dioxin	0.00000003
Endrin (organic)	0.002
Fluoride	4.0
Foaming agents	0.5
Iron (>0.3 makes red water)	0.3
Lead	0.015
Lindane (organic)	0.0002
Manganese (>0.1 forms brown-black stains)	0.05
Mercury	0.002
Methoxychlor (organic)	0.04
Nitrate	10.0
Odor (threshold odor)	3.0
p-Dichlorobenzene (organic)	0.075
pH	6.5-8.5
Radium -226 and -228	5pCi/L
Selenium	0.05
Silver	0.1
Sulfate (>500 has a laxative effect)	250.0
Total dissolved solids	500.0
Toxaphene (organic)	0.003
1,1,1 Trichloroethane (organic)	0.2
Trichloroethane (organic)	0.005
Trihalomethanes (organic)	0.1
Turbidity (silica scale)	1 to 5 TU
Uranium	30_g/L
Vinyl chloride (organic)	0.002
Zinc	5.0
2,4-D (organic)	0.07

Published by Milestone. Copyright protected.

0-7696-3429-X *Science Fair Projects: Volume 2*